SOUTH WEST COAST PATH

Padstow to Falmouth

NATIONAL TRAIL GUIDES

SOUTH WEST COAST PATH

Padstow to Falmouth

John Macadam

Photographs by
Mike Williams

Aurum

in association with

NATURAL
ENGLAND

Acknowledgements

I am indebted to many people who have provided information and photographs for this book. For this latest edition I have particularly benefited from help by Mark Owen of the South West Coast Path Team, Dave Barnett, Claire Mucklow and Dr Bren Unwin. It is also opportune to thank another walker, Piers Burnett, of Aurum Press, who it has been a pleasure to work with over the years.

John Macadam was brought up in Devon, and has been using the Coast Path since 1965. Since 1972 he has lived in Cornwall, working as a lecturer, and writing about the environment under the 'Earthwords' banner. He is past chairman of the geological conservation group of the Cornwall Wildlife Trust, and a member of the Outdoor Writers' and Photographers' Guild.

This revised edition first published 2009 by Aurum Press Ltd
in association with Natural England

Text copyright © 1990, 1996, 2000, 2002, 2005, 2007, 2009 by Aurum Press Ltd
and Natural England

The photographs are copyright © Natural England and are by Mike Williams except for page 62 (Simon Cook) and 106 (Paul Glendell). Other photographs are by:
John Macadam (page 65); Bren Unwin (pages 12, 31, 32, 55, 69, 87 and 92);
National Trust/Tony Kent (page 43); National Trust/Dave Flunder (page 120),
National Trust/Jane Gifford (page 134); and Jamie MacArthur (page 113).

John Dehane Macadam has asserted his rights under Section 77 of the Copyright, Designs and Patents Act 1988 to be identified as the author of this work.

Book design by Robert Updegraff
Printed and bound in Italy by Printer Trento Srl

Cover photograph: *Wheal Coates, part of the Cornish Mining World Heritage Site (National Trust photograph)*
Title page photograph: *St Michael's Mount*

CONTENTS

HOW TO USE THIS GUIDE

The 630-mile (1008-kilometre) South West Coast Path is covered by four National Trail guides. This book describes the Coast Path from Padstow to Falmouth, 169 miles (271 kilometres). Companion guides describe the Coast Path from Minehead to Padstow, from Falmouth to Exmouth, and from Exmouth to Poole. Each guide therefore covers a section of the Coast Path between major estuaries, where walkers may need a ferry or other transport.

This guide is in three parts:

• The introduction, general information about the South West Coast Path and advice for walkers.

• The Coast Path itself, described in thirteen chapters, with maps accompanying each section of the route description. This text also includes information on places or features of interest or historical importance and descriptions of attractive towns and villages 'JUST OFF THE PATH'. Key sites are numbered or lettered in the text and on the maps to make it easy to follow the route description.

• The last part includes useful information, such as local transport, ferries and river crossings, accommodation and further reading.

The maps have been prepared by the Ordnance Survey using 1:25 000 Explorer® maps as a base. The line of the Coast Path is shown in yellow with the status of each section – footpath or bridleway for example – shown in green underneath (see key on inside front cover). In some cases the yellow line on these maps may show a route which is different from that shown on older maps. Walkers are then recommended to follow the yellow route in this guide, which is that waymarked with the distinctive acorn symbol 🌰 used for all National Trails. Any parts of the Coast Path that may be difficult to follow on the ground are clearly highlighted in the route description, and important points to watch for are marked with letters in each chapter, both in the text and on the maps. *Black arrows (➡) at the edge of the maps indicate the start point.* **Should there have been a need to alter the route since the publication of this guide, walkers are advised to follow the signs which have been erected on site to indicate this.**

KEY MAP 2

Godrevy Island

Navax Point

Cra

Kel

Gwithian

Rosewort

The Carracks

South West Coast Path

St Ives Bay

ST IVES

Carbis Bay

The Towans

Phillack

Connor Do

Angarrack

Gwinear

B3306

Gurnard's Head

Zennor

Boswednack

247 Halsetown

Trendrine Hill

Towednack

Longstone

Copperhouse

Hayle

St Erth

Praze

Realwa

Pendeen Watch

Morvah

Lower Boscaswell

Trewellard

Higher Bojewyan

Pendeen

Botallack

Carnyorth

Cape Cornwall

The Brisons

St Just

Tregeseal

Newbridge

Porthmeor

252

Boskednan

Cripplesease

Georgia

Chysauster

Nancledra

Canon's Town

163

St Erth

Great Bosullow

Madron

New Mill

Ludgvan

Crowlas

B3302

Townsh

A30

River Ha

St Hilary

Golsithney

Relubbus House

Trescowe

194

Heamoor

Chyandour

Marazion

Higher Downs

Perran Downs

Germoe

Tregonn

Ashton Hill

Lands End (St Just) Aerodrome

Tremethick Cross

Grumbla

Sancreed

Kelynack

Bosavern

Ancient Village

Brane

Drift Res

A30

Drift

PENZANCE

St Michael's Mount

Perranuthnoe

Rosudgeon

Praa Sands

Carn Towan

Croes-an-wra

Tredavoe

Kerris

NEWLYN

Paul

Mousehole

Cudden Point

Rinsey

Whitesand Bay

Sennen Cove

Sennen

St Buryan

St Clement's Isle

Welloe

Trewavas Head

ngships

LAND'S END

Castallack

MOUNT'S BAY

Porth

Lamorna

Trethewey

Porthcurno

Treen

Cribba Head

Logan Rock

South West Coast Path

Gwennap Head

St Levan

Runnel Stone

Pendeen

Trewellard

Botallack

B318

A3071

A394

A3071

B3306

B3301

B3311

B3283

B3315

B3315

13

7

9

8

6

10

| 0 km | | 5 |
| 0 miles | | 5 |

Distance checklist

This list will assist you in calculating the distances between places on the Coast Path where you may be planning to stay overnight, or in checking your progress along the way.

location	*approx. distance from previous location*	
	miles	*km*
Padstow	0	0
Treyarnon Bay Youth Hostel	11.4	18.3
Mawgan Porth	6.6	10.7
Newquay (station)	5.8	9.3
Crantock (by tidal bridge)	4.1	6.6
Perranporth	8.5	13.6
Trevaunance Cove (for St Agnes)	3.9	6.3
Portreath	8.5	13.6
Gwithian	7.6	12.2
Hayle	4.1	6.7
St Ives	6.1	9.8
Zennor Head (for Zennor)	6.5	10.4
Pendeen Watch (for Pendeen)	7.2	11.6
Cape Cornwall (for St Just)	4.0	6.4
Sennen Cove	5.1	8.3
Land's End	1.2	2.0
Porthcurno	5.0	8.1
Lamorna Cove	5.4	8.7
Mousehole	2.4	3.9
Penzance	3.6	5.9
Marazion	3.1	5.0
Praa Sands	6.3	10.2
Porthleven	4.4	7.2
Polurrian Cove (for Mullion)	6.3	10.2
Lizard Point (for Lizard Town)	7.7	12.4
Cadgwith	3.5	5.6
Coverack	6.9	11.1
Porthoustock	3.6	5.9
Gillan	4.0	6.5
St Antony-in-Meneage (by road)	2.1	3.5
Helford	2.9	4.8
Helford Passage (by road and paths)	8.4	13.5
Falmouth (Albert Quay)	10.0	16.0

PREFACE

The South West Coast Path National Trail is a 630-mile (1008-km) adventure around the coastline of the south-west peninsula. From Minehead on the edge of the Exmoor National Park all the way to the shores of Poole Harbour, it is simply the best way to enjoy this wonderful coastline, its scenery, wildlife and history.

Between Padstow and Falmouth the Trail takes in mainland Britain's most south-westerly and southerly points (Land's End and the Lizard) before reaching the Fal Estuary, its largest natural harbour. Along the way, there are dramatic cliffs and headlands and the contrasting estuaries of the north and south coasts. Some are crossed by ferry and others on foot at some stages of the tide. Either experience will add an extra dimension to your Coast Path walk.

Following the Coast Path you can go at your own pace, enjoying the changing landscape and wildlife and getting the feel of how people have lived and worked in the coastal corridor down the centuries. In many places you will come across the evidence of Cornwall's industrial past. The mining landscapes around St Agnes and St Just, together with the port of Hayle, now form part of the Cornish Mining World Heritage Site, inscribed in 2006. You may also stop off at busy towns and villages, bustling resorts, beaches or sheltered coves – each with its own character.

Natural England is proud of its role in creating and being the major funder of the South West Coast Path. The Path is maintained by local authorities, working with other organisations such as the National Trust where appropriate. One of the family of 15 National Trails in England and Wales, the Coast Path is clearly signed with the acorn waymark. It is enjoyed by millions of people every year, both local residents and visitors, and offers relaxation and challenge, tranquillity and inspiration. Whether you are about to stroll out along the cliffs from Cape Cornwall or Lizard Point, or walk all the way from Padstow to Falmouth, I hope you too will discover – or rediscover – the endless fascination of the South West Coast Path.

Martin Doughty
Chair
Natural England

This is a walk for those who like salty air. Sometimes you may even be surrounded by flying foam. It is not pollution!

PART ONE

INTRODUCTION

INTRODUCTION

by John Macadam

On the edge of the land

The South West Coast Path must be one of the most spectacular and varied long-distance trails in the world. And at 630 miles (just over 1000 kilometres), from Minehead to Poole, it is certainly Britain's longest. Never far from the sea, the route will take the walker high above the shore and then swoop down to a fishing village in a cove. In fact, someone has calculated that if you walk those 630 miles, you will also climb three times the height of Everest! Not that you will need extra oxygen, of course, though windproof insulated clothing can be much appreciated if you are walking into a sou'westerly gale. At other times a T-shirt is more appropriate. But more about that later.

The trail will take you through historic towns and villages, through woods, fields and sand dunes, and alongside quiet creeks and past streams falling from high cliffs into the sea. Occasionally you will walk through a busy town, but often there will be more wildlife – the inevitable gulls, but maybe also seals, basking sharks, dolphins or choughs – than humans. To refresh yourself there are local beers, clotted-cream teas, Cornish pasties, Ruby Red steaks and Dorset Blue cheese, and smoked mackerel. Or you could sample the industrial heritage: pilchard 'palaces' and mining in Cornwall, or quarrying on Portland. If none of that takes your fancy, there are more ethereal pleasures: literary associations, from Daniel Defoe to John Fowles, connections with artists from Turner to Kurt Jackson, the Cornish language ('Kernewek') and innumerable Celtic saints. And if you do not like beer, there's a range of ciders made from traditional varieties of apples in Somerset and Devon, and even a few recently planted vineyards near the Path.

For centuries, local people used paths along the coast for many purposes, including gathering food and looking for wreckage. But in the 18th century the government imposed high import duties on a range of luxury goods, precipitating a rapid growth in smuggling – and yet another use for the paths. The official response was draconian legislation prohibiting anyone from 'lurking, waiting or loitering within five miles from the sea-coast', but the trade was too lucrative to suppress. Finally, in the early 19th century, the coastguard service was set up, with men patrolling nightly, and so a continuous coast path developed. The coastguards had to be able to look down into coves and narrow inlets, so their route was truly at the edge of the cliffs. But by the early 1800s, a few visitors were using the path for leisure, even if they sometimes had to prove that they had no other purpose!

Use of much of this path was lost, not, as might be expected, by natural geological processes, but by landowners, often backed by the courts, prohibiting access. In 1949 the Act which set up National Parks in England and Wales also set up long-distance paths, including one around the South West Peninsula. The Path was opened in stages, with the last major section opened in 1978, and the patient operation to reinstate the route along the coast is now nearly complete.

Geological processes have indeed destroyed the old coast-guards' tracks in many places, and those same processes are no respecters of hard-won modern routes, so realignment is an ongoing task. Active erosion also means that the geology is exposed in many places, not clothed in soil and vegetation as

The convoluted coastline at Merope Island is the result of complex geology, fretted away by the sea.

It is best to find out tide times so you can work out where you can cross the Gannel Estua

Cligga Mine is part of the Cornish Mining Landscape World Heritage Site, though the round buddles in this picture only date back to the Second World War.

inland, so the walker will see an impressive range of strata, folds, faults, intrusions, ore veins, stacks and caves – a real *tour de force*.

Uniquely among the National Trails, the Path passes through two World Heritage Sites: the 95 miles of 'Jurassic Coast' in East Devon and Dorset and the Cornish Mining Landscape. Moreover, the designation of these sites by UNESCO was only the icing on the cake, for much of the Path passes through areas with one or more national designations for landscape, wildlife or geology: National Park, National Nature Reserve, Heritage Coast, Area of Outstanding Natural Beauty, Site of Special Scientific Interest, and others. But you do not have to be an expert (or understand all these designations!) to enjoy all the flowers, butterflies and birds you will see at different times of the year.

Management of the Path requires great sensitivity to potentially competing interests. Funded primarily by Natural England, this task is shared between approximately 70 staff working for six highway authorities (or their agents), the Ministry of Defence, and the National Trust, and co-ordinated by the South West Coast Path Team based in Exeter. Day-to-day work includes cutting back vegetation, clearing drainage ditches, and replacing broken stiles and signs. In addition to routine maintenance, South West Coast Path managers aim to provide the best experience by realigning sections that involve road walking or re-routing the Path as quickly as possible after cliff-falls have taken place.

Planning your walk

You may be planning to walk the whole length of the Path, or you may just intend to walk a short distance. Even a walk along the promenade is likely to be a walk along the Coast Path! Some of the Path can be enjoyed by people who are less mobile, but very little can be used by cyclists or horse-riders.

If you are planning short walks, there are many circular routes to get you back to your starting point, and in many places there is public transport (but make sure you take the bus or train to your furthest point, then walk back, or else leave yourself plenty of time).

Whatever walk you plan, be sure you are fit enough, particularly if you are planning to walk for several days consecutively. Remember those four Everests! Some people walk the whole Path in one go, and most take 50–60 days to do this. A few people have taken far less time, but they must have missed out a great deal.

The best time to walk the Path is probably May–June, with long days, masses of wild flowers and few people. Another good time is September, when most of the summer visitors have gone. Since the area relies heavily on tourism, there is a wide range of accommodation, from campsites, youth hostels, B&Bs (bed & breakfast) to rather grand hotels, though everywhere can become full at the height of the tourist season in July and August and it is wise to book ahead. If you intend to camp away from a recognised campsite, you will need to ask permission of the landowner, usually the local farmer, and remember to leave no trace of your stay.

If you plan to walk between October and April, you may have the luxury of the Coast Path to yourself. You may also find some ferries are not running and public services, like buses and trains, are running a restricted winter schedule. Tourist Information Centres (TICs), the information section at the back of this book and the National Trail website (www.nationaltrail.co.uk) will either provide the necessary information or give you the necessary contacts.

Wild carrot flowers beside the Path in late summer near Rinsey Head.

Equipment

British weather is notorious for its changeability, and the weather in the South West is generally wetter, windier and warmer than most of Britain. Most of the Coast Path is very exposed to the elements; the exceptions are some of the estuaries. The relative exposure depends on which way the wind is coming from – the prevailing wind is southwesterly – and which way the coast faces. The effects of windchill can be extreme: windchill is caused by the wind evaporating moisture from your skin.

With all this in mind, it makes sense to get a weather forecast (from the media, by telephone or the web) and be prepared. It is always sensible to carry a windproof waterproof: the breathable ones are best, and the reproofable ones with a lifetime guarantee are the best of all.

There are various types of walking trousers, though most people use quick-drying polycotton fabrics, with waterproof

overtrousers. Denim is decidedly unwise as when wet it becomes stiff and heavy, and is also very slow to dry, thus increasing the risk of hypothermia. A hat of some form is recommended, and a supply of sunscreen to be applied in good time to your neck, arms and anywhere else that is exposed. Traditionally, strong shoes or walking boots with good grips have always been recommended, though some people are very happy wearing sandals designed for walkers.

Finally, walkers need to take an adequate supply of liquid, a whistle and a first-aid kit, all in a rucksack which is adjusted to fit the wearer comfortably. Of course, long-distance walkers will have far more to carry than this, but will take trouble to minimise the weight. Some companies and B&B owners will transport your pack for you to your next stop, for a fee, so that all you need to carry is a daypack. Cash machines are only to be found in the larger towns, so paying bills and withdrawing cash can be a problem, especially for visitors without a sterling cheque account.

Finding your way

The sign for all National Trails is a stylised acorn, and you will find this cut into wooden waymarks, chiselled into stone way-marks, cast in metal, and stuck to aluminium road signs. Most signs also bear the words 'Coast Path'.

You should have few problems following the acorns and thus the trail. The route is also shown on the maps in this guidebook. You may find that the route has changed from that shown on the maps, in which case follow the acorns and any diversion signs. The reason for the latter may well be a cliff-fall, or the Path starting to crumble away. It is obviously foolhardy to ignore diversion signs.

Safety

The main safety message is: keep to the Path. The Path is close to the cliff edge in many places. Make sure you are suitably equipped both for your walk and for changing weather conditions.

Those who go down to beaches and rocks beside the sea need to be aware of the tides, with around 9 metres between high and low tide at Minehead, though only a couple of metres at Poole. Every year people get cut off by the tide and have to be rescued. People also get washed off rocks by so-called 'freak waves'. At many places around this coastline you can watch surfers waiting for the bigger waves.

Bathing too can be hazardous, chiefly because of currents. It is best only to swim in safe areas patrolled by lifeguards, who are employed only in the summer. Many beaches have rip currents which drain most of the water that comes onto the beach. If you get caught in a rip current, do not try to swim against it, but rather swim diagonally across it until you are in stiller water, when it is safe to swim back to the beach.

If you do get into difficulties, the international alarm call is six long blasts on a whistle, followed by one minute's silence.

The coastguards are responsible for dealing with any emergency that occurs on the coast or at sea. Please remember that there are no coastguard lookouts now, and the service relies on the watchful eyes of the public. If you see vessels or people you think are in distress, dial 999 (or 112 on a mobile) and ask for the coastguard. In some places there may be no mobile signal.

The Act forbidding 'lurking, waiting or loitering within five miles from the sea-coast' was repealed in 1825, so relax, explore and enjoy the South West Coast Path and the coasts of Somerset, Devon, Cornwall and Dorset.

PART TWO

SOUTH WEST COAST PATH
Padstow to Falmouth

1 Padstow to Treyarnon Bay

via Trevone and Trevose Head
11.4 miles (18.3 km)

This is an easy walk, much of it along low cliffs at the back of popular beaches. If you have crossed the Camel Estuary, the ferry will normally have dropped you at North Quay **1** in Padstow, but if the tide was low you will be left at Lower Beach **2**. There is information on all the ferries used along the route on pages 137–39.

The Coast Path leaves the harbour by the slope **A** beside the discreet red brick toilets on North Quay Parade. The tarmac path continues to a modern granite cross, the war memorial, passing a notice pointing out that the ferry crosses at low tide from Lower Beach, which is down a track and then steps. Beyond the war memorial the path is a veritable highway to the very sheltered St George's Cove **3**.

Gun Point **4** has a bolted cast-iron water tank dated 1888 and a war-department granite marker dated 1868, but was already called Gun Point on the Ordnance Survey Map of 1801. The site is listed, among others, as being fortified against the Armada, although it is not known if this was ever carried out.

The Coast Path is carried on boards through the marsh at the head of Harbour Cove **5**. This area, where marsh orchids now grow, had moorings for boats in the 1920s before the main channel of the Camel straightened, going north from Gun Point to Trebetherick Point on the eastern side. If the tide is out you can cross the dunes and the good sandy beach at Harbour Cove, known locally as Tregirls.

The changing sand banks in the estuary led to the removal of the lifeboat from its base at Hawker's Cove. The path skirts the converted lifeboat house and joins the road for a few yards at the back of the beach. The older terrace, with chimneys set at an angle, was built in 1874 for the pilots, while the newer houses, made of white brick from North Devon, were used by the coastguards. In order to help vessels make the safety of Padstow without being driven on to the Doom Bar, capstans were installed in the lee of Stepper Point and ships warped round. The outline of Stepper has been much altered by quarrying.

As you leave the sheltered side of the estuary and start the walk down the coast, the change in scenery is dramatic. A little way on, and in spring among a carpet of squill, is a stone tower **6**, built in 1832 by the Association for the Preservation of Life and Property as a daymark to help guide ships into the Camel.

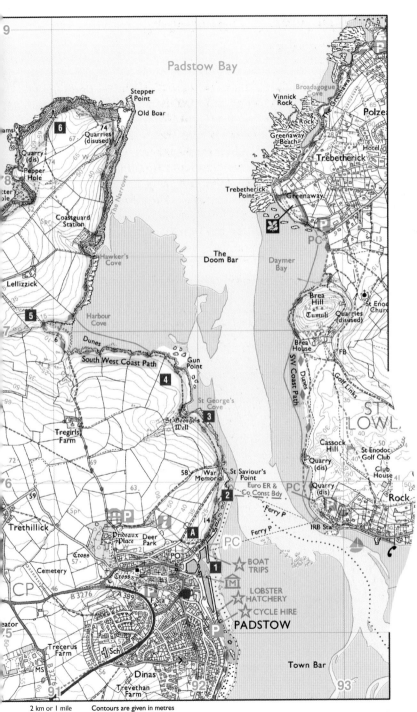

Padstow Bay

Stepper
Point

Old Boar

6

74
Quarries
(disused)

ams

Quarry
(dis)

Pepper
Hole

8

The Narrows

Coastguard
Station

Hawker's
Cove

The
Doom Bar

Daymer
Bay

Lellizzick

5

Harbour
Cove

Dunes

South West Coast Path

Gun
Point

4

Tregirls
Farm

St George's
Cove

St George's
Well

3

War
Memorial

58

St Saviour's
Point

2

63

Euro ER &
Co Const Bdy

Ferry P

Trethillick

14

A

Ferry P

IRB Sta

Cross

PO

PC

Cemetery

Cross

1 ☆ **BOAT
TRIPS**

P Sta

🅼 **LOBSTER
HATCHERY**

☆ **CYCLE HIRE**

CP

B 3276

A 389

P

PADSTOW

Trecerus
Farm

Sch

eator

MS

Dinas

Town Bar

Trevethan
Farm

91

92

93

Vinnick
Rock

Broadagogue
Cove

Shag
Rock

The Greenaway

Polze

Greenaway
Beach

Trebetherick

Hotel

Trebetherick
Point

Greenaway

P

PC

Brea
Hill

St Enod
Church

Tumuli

Quarries
(disused)

Brea
House

FB

SW Coast Path

Dunes

Golf Links

ST
LOWL

Cassock
Hill

St Enodoc
Golf Club

Quarry
(dis)

Club
House

Quarry
(dis)

Rock

Near Merope Islands **7** is the first of many mines you will pass before Falmouth, but only some vegetated dumps remain.

Most of the rock along the coast in North Cornwall is slate, of Devonian age, apart from occasional igneous rock headlands, but at Marble Cliffs **8**, Porthmissen, there is limestone – a rarity here. There are more than 80 beds of limestone with shale between the layers, just as in the much younger Jurassic Lias, found in a belt from Lyme Regis in Dorset to Whitby in Yorkshire, but here there are no ammonites or ichthyosaurs, and the whole sequence is upside-down, as well as being very localised. Razorbills, guillemots, kittiwakes and fulmars nest on the limestone layers. Another nearby geological curiosity is the Round Hole, a collapsed sea cave. Trevone is useful for walkers, with its post office and shop, accommodation and pub, and it is also on the Padstow–Newquay bus route which links the villages along the coast. Further on, people in wheelchairs can now enjoy the view from Newtrain Bay and St Cadoc's Point **9**. Under Harlyn Inn is

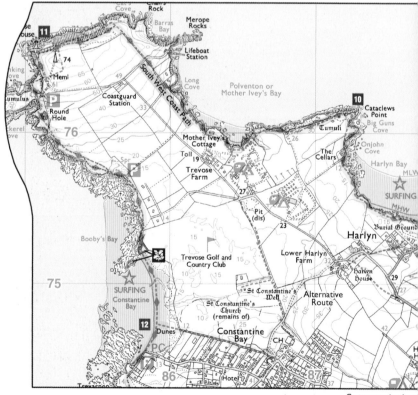

Contours are given in me
The vertical interval is 5

the site of an Iron Age cemetery that held over 100 crouched skeletons; the finds from the area are now in Truro museum.

The path westwards from Harlyn Bridge currently follows the beach for a short distance, but at the highest spring tides it may be necessary to go inland along the road through the hamlet of Harlyn to the village of Constantine Bay, then take the path to the beach at Constantine Bay **12**. The Cellars are old fish cellars and date from the days when Harlyn Bay was the site of a pilchard seine. The inscription over the (blocked-up) door – LUCRI DULCIS ODOR – can be translated as 'Sweet is the smell of riches'! More information on pilchards can be found on page 39.

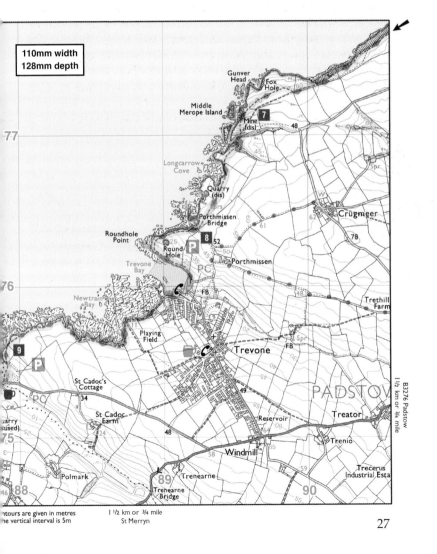

ntours are given in metres
he vertical interval is 5m   1 ½ km or ¾ mile
St Merryn   27

The old quarries **10** at Cataclews Point are now the site of a sewage treatment works. The distinctive Cataclews stone was used by the Master of St Endellion in the 14th century to carve the fonts in Padstow and St Merryn churches. The stone is a variety of dolerite, a rock often called 'blue elvan' by Cornish quarrymen, to distinguish it from the usual 'elvan', which is a fine-grained granite often associated with metal lodes and also used for carving.

Another dolerite forms Merope Rocks, where ravens nest and which shelters Padstow's new lifeboat station. Before the move to Mother Ivey's Bay in 1967, Padstow had lost three lifeboats on the Doom Bar. This station, like nearly all the others between here and Falmouth, is open to visitors, and you can find out more from www.rnli.org.uk.

Trevose Head Lighthouse **11** was opened in 1847 to fill in the gap between the Longships and the old Lundy light. The light is now automated and the keepers' cottages are holiday lets. The path now turns south, crossing the back of the beach at Constantine Bay **12**. Swimming can be hazardous both here and at Treyarnon Bay **13**, where there is a youth hostel with a café, a caravan site, and a hotel.

Padstow

'This is one of those antiquated unsavoury fishing-towns which are viewed most agreeably from a distance', according to Murray's 1859 *Guide to Devon and Cornwall*. The reeking pilchard palaces are long disused, but Padstow is still a fishing town, with most of the activity on the southern side of the harbour. In summer the town is crowded with visitors but is still a pleasantly antiquated place to explore out of season. St Petroc, a much revered Welsh missionary, founded a monastery here in the 7th century, which was moved to Bodmin in 981 after a Viking raid.

The Camel Estuary forms a rare natural harbour on the dangerous north Cornish coast, and Padstow grew as a centre for shipbuilding, trade and fishing. The safety of the harbour became illusory, however, because of the growth of the great sand bar, the Doom Bar, at its mouth, on which 300 vessels are known to have been wrecked or stranded in the 150 years to the beginning of last century, and countless more before. The sand is composed of broken shells, so hundreds of thousands of tons were taken away to improve the sour acidic soils of Cornwall, although today crushed limestone from upcountry has largely replaced the shell sand.

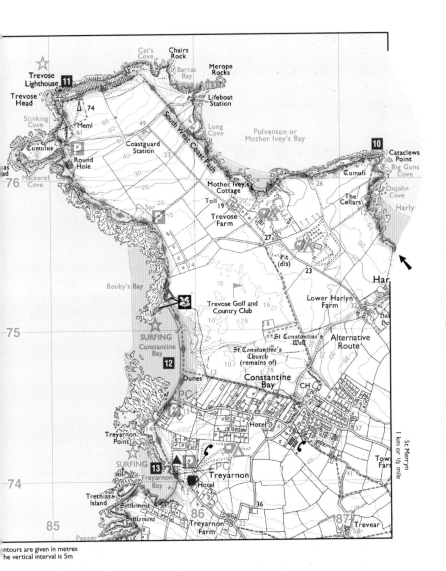

ntours are given in metres
he vertical interval is 5m

Nowadays Padstow is best known for its 'Obby 'Osses on May Day. Even St Petroc, St Wethinoc, St Samson and St Cadoc might not be able to dampen the pagan gusto of this celebration of the return of summer. A former lord of the manor did once try to bribe the local people – with a roast ox – if they desisted. His descendants still live in Prideaux Place but have a different attitude. Should you visit this Elizabethan house, you may have a sense of *déjà vu*: it has been used in several films.

Cornish place names and the Cornish language

Near the River Tamar, the boundary between the counties of Devon and Cornwall, many of the place names are of English (i.e. Anglo-Saxon) origin, but further west Cornish takes the place of English, and by the time the Land's End peninsula is reached non-Cornish names are a rarity. Thus most of the place names encountered on this part of the coast are of Cornish origin, though both 'Padstow' and 'Falmouth' are English. The earliest name recorded for Padstow is 'Sancte Petroces Stow', the holy place of St Petroc (Pedrek), in 981, while the earliest references to 'Falemouth' and 'Fallmouth' date from the 15th century. Cornwall itself is 'Kernow' in Cornish, and is thought to originate from the name of a tribe called the Cornowii or 'horn-people', possibly because they lived at the end of the peninsula. Many places are self-evidently named after saints, for example St Ives (St Ia), but with many others the 'saint' has been dropped: examples are Zennor, Constantine, Gwithian, Paul, Gunwalloe and Gwennap. Various descriptive words are common in Cornish place names, for example:

als/alt	cliff	loe/logh	lake, sheltered inlet
bal	mine	los	grey
bean/vean	small	lyn	lake
bos/bod	dwelling	maen	stone
bre	hill	meneth	hill
carn	tor, rock, crag	meur/veor	great, big
carrek	rock	mor	sea
castel	fort	nans/nant	valley
chi/chy/ty	house, cottage	ogo/fougou	cave
dhu/du	black	penn/pen/pedn	head, end, top
dinas	fort	poll/pol	pool, cove
dowr	water, stream	pons/pont	bridge
eglos	church	porth	cove, harbour
fenten/venton	spring	ros	moor, promontory
glas/las	green, blue	rys/rid	ford
goeles/wollas	lower	sawn/zawn	cleft, gully
goon/noon	down, moorland	sten	tin
gwartha/wartha	upper	tewynn/towan	sand dunes
gwin/gwidden	white	tir/tyr	land
hal	wet moor	tre(v)	farmstead, hamlet
hen	old	treth	beach
heyl/hayle	estuary	wheal	mine
kew/gew	hollow	ynys/enys	island, isolated place
lan/lann	church site		

The twentieth century saw a revival in the Cornish language, and it is possible to learn it at evening classes and even in some schools. Kernewek (Cornish) is now recognised as a minority language in Europe. In many churches the Lord's Prayer in Cornish hangs on the wall, and occasional services are conducted in the language. But despite this revival the language is no longer in everyday use. The last native Cornish speaker is reputed to have been Dolly Pentreath, a 'jowster' or fish hawker of Mousehole, who died in 1777, although at Zennor there is a memorial to John Davey, the last person with any traditional knowledge of Cornish, who died in 1891. Certainly 1800 is accepted as about the latest date at which Cornish was in use by anyone as a living language, after a decline dating back to the first incursions of the Anglo-Saxons across the Tamar, probably in the 8th century.

The Men-an-Tol, the 'stone with a hole', is one of the many archaeological sites you can reach by bus from the Coast Path.

2 Treyarnon Bay to Newquay

via Mawgan Porth and Griffin's Point
12.5 miles (20 km)

The route to Newquay is mostly easy, right on the edge of flat-topped cliffs, from where you look down on a spectacular range of coves, caves and stacks. Treyarnon Bay **13** is very dangerous for swimming at low water because of a strong current, which will take you out to sea, so instead use the 'swimming pool' in the rocks on the north-east side.

Immediately south of Trethias Island are what appear to be three Iron Age cliff castles **14**, which in fact are one, but erosion has cut the coves, and separated the defensive bank into three sections. Erosion is still proceeding rapidly, so take care. The remains of the *Hemsley I* are visible at low tide in Fox Cove. She was an aged tanker on her last voyage to the breaker's yard at Antwerp when she struck in a gale in 1969 and sank.

Soon the path turns inland to Porthcothan, which has suffered rather lopsided development; the northern side is owned by the National Trust (NT) and has not been built on. The route follows the road for a few yards, then turns back to the beach past a useful shop. There is also a pub, phone box, public conveniences and a bus stop.

The path skirts the seaward side of the houses towards Trescore Islands. In one small cove **15** there are some man-made caves, and various spikes embedded in the rock: relics of smuggling, or of unloading and dismembering a wreck? Park Head **16**, owned by the NT, has a spectacularly sited cliff castle, as well as a large area slipping in stages down to the beach and into the sea.

Iron rings along the Path may be associated with mining, smuggling or wrecking.

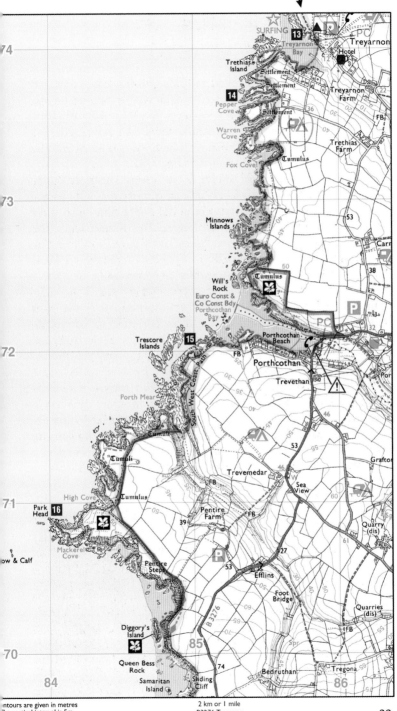

SURFING

Treyarnon

13

Treyarnon
Bay

Hotel

Treyarnon
Farm

Trethias
Island

Settlement

Settlement

FB

74

Pepper
Cove

14

Settlement

Warren
Cove

Trethias
Farm

Fox Cove

Tumulus

Carn

53

73

Minnows
Islands

38

50

Will's
Rock

Tumulus

Euro Const &
Co Const Bdy
Porthcothan
Bay

P

PC

Trescore
Islands

15

Porthcothan
Beach

72

FB

Porthcothan

South West Coast Path

Porth Mear

Trevethan

!

Tumulus

Tumuli

Trevemedar

53

Grafton

46

High Cove

Tumulus

FB

Sea
View

71

Park
Head

16

Pentire
Farm

FB

Quarry
(dis)

39

ow & Calf

Mackerel
Cove

P

27

Pentire
Steps

53

Efflins

Foot
Bridge

Quarries
(dis)

Diggory's
Island

85

FB

B 3276

70

Queen Bess
Rock

Samaritan
Island

74

Sliding
Cliff

Bedruthan

Tregona

84

86

Park Head attracts a few visitors, those who like fresh air and spectacular views, but Bedruthan Steps **17** is a tourist honey-pot. The Steps are owned by the Carnanton Estate and were developed as a tourist attraction by the Victorians after the railway reached Newquay in 1875. The NT has a property called Carnewas to the south and has tackled the erosion problem there by building a path leading to a viewing platform looking out over the Steps, which are closed in winter. The NT car park is surrounded by a Cornish hedge, rock-faced with an earthern core. There is also a small shop and a deservedly popular tea shop open from spring to autumn. The slate stacks include Queen Bess, who lost her head a few years ago, as you will realise if you see old photographs, and Samaritan Island, the site of the wreck of a ship called the *Samaritan*, which indeed gave succour to the local population.

The path descends from Trenance Point to Mawgan Porth past a strange linear depression **18** in which two garden sheds and a greenhouse nestle. This depression is part of a canal intended to link Mawgan Porth, St Columb and Porth (now part of Newquay) and to carry mainly sea-sand to 'afford the means of improving many thousand acres of barren and unprofitable ground'. It was also intended to carry coal inland and St Columb stone for export. The canal was never finished, although the section from Trenance to St Columb was completed by 1779.

Mawgan Porth has a car park, toilets, shops, hotels and a bus service. Up the valley is the village of St Mawgan with some of the best memorial brasses in Cornwall in the church. Nearby is Newquay Airport, Cornwall's main airport which also has a military side. The Coast Path joins the beach at the northern end of the dunes **A**.

Griffin's Point **19** has a well-preserved cliff castle into which the path just cuts. Many of the headlands in the south-west have cliff castles, which are also known as promontory forts and which date from the Iron Age, approximately the 4th century BC to the Romano-British time.

The path now starts the long sweep of Watergate Bay, which ends in Newquay. The bay is sandy and good for surfing and many other sports. The rocks are the oldest on the path between Padstow and Falmouth (apart from the Lizard). They contain fragments of early jawless fish almost 400 million years old, which appear to have sucked up their food from the bottom of rivers and lakes.

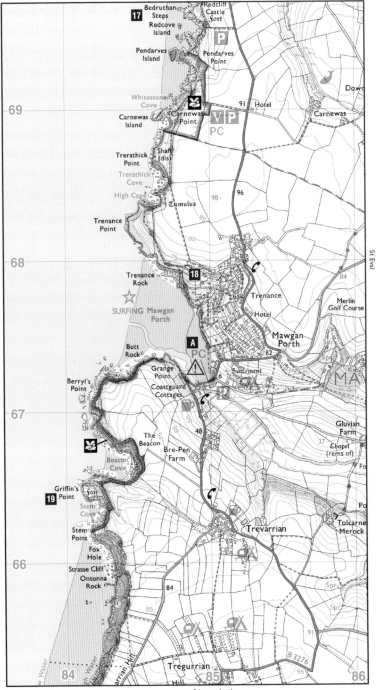

Bedruthan Steps
17
Redcove Island
Redcliff Castle Fort
Pendarves Island
Pendarves Point
P
Whitestone Cove
91 Hotel
Carnewas
69
Carnewas Island
Carnewas Point
VP
PC
Trerathick Point
Shaft (dis)
Trerathick Cove
High Cove
98·   96
Tumulus
95
Trenance Point
90
75
68
Trenance Rock
18
84
SURFING Mawgan Porth
Trenance
Merlin Golf Course
Hotel
Butt Rock
A
Mawgan Porth
PC
Grange Point
62
Berryl's Point
⚠
Coastguard Cottages
6
Settlement
MA
The Beacon
48
Gluvian Farm
67
Beacon Cove
Bre-Pen Farm
37
Chapel (rems of)
Fo
Griffin's Point
Fort
19
Stem Cove
Tolcarne Merock
Po
Stem Point
Trevarrian
Fox Hole
Strasse Cliff
Ontonna Rock
66
84
85
91
B 3276
84
Tregurrian
85
95
86

St. Eval

Down

Carnewas

Spr

Spr

The path snakes around two large tumuli and then descends to Porth, passing Trevelgue Head, the most heavily defended cliff castle in Cornwall, leading archaeologists to suspect that before Porth silted up it was an important landing place. As well as the seven ramparts, evidence of bronze and iron smelting has been found and the site was occupied, discontinuously, from at least the 3rd century BC to the 6th century AD.

You must now follow a short stretch of road, passing The Mermaid pub, guarded by a 12-pounder gun – naval pattern of course. The next ancient site is Barrowfields **20**, so called because of the three Bronze Age barrows. Then follow the road until you reach the pedestrian and cycle way, the Tram Track **B**, leading seawards shortly after the railway station. Continue along Bank Street and Fore Street to North Quay Hill and the harbour **21**.

Nowadays Newquay is a lively holiday town, but its history includes the pilchard fishery and silver-lead mining, and it was the industrial port for the Treffry family, one of the major families involved in the development of the china clay industry. Newquay has many places to eat and to stay, post offices, banks, trains and buses, but if your prefererence is for quiet walks on moonlit beaches you may choose to stay elsewhere.

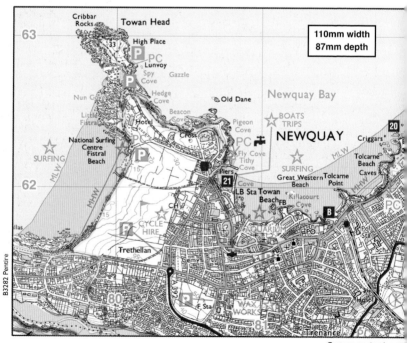

Contours are given in metr
The vertical interval is 5m

Watergate Bay

SURFING Hotel

Trevarrian Hill

Tre

PC

Tregurrian

The White House

Mean Low Water
Mean High Water

65

Trevarrian Run

P

Tinner's Point

Creepinghole Point

Twr

69

Horse Rock

Sweden Rock

Fruitful Cove

64

Trebelsue Farm

Zacry's Islands

South West Coast Path

Watergate Road

Spr

Tumuli

Fern Cavern

Trevelgue Court

Sewage Works

Whipsiderry Beach

54 Hotel

32

Tregu Farm

Black Humphrey Rock or Flory Island

P

Trevelgue Head

Dollar Rock

Whipsiderry

Tumulus

63 Porth Island

FB

Fort

Penrose

Wine Cove

Hotel

Porth Beach

PC

Porth

NEWQUAY CP

Priory Road

Caves

Lusty Glaze

Playing Fields

wfields

St Columb Minor

62

Coll

48 Playing Field

Sch

Recn Gd

Sch

Cemy

PO

Rialton Road

A 3059

Tretherras

26

Gusti Veor

MS

Chy an Gover

25

Quintrell Road

A 3059

Trenance eisure Park

83

Spr

84

Trewollac Farm

57

A 3059 St Columb Major
7 km or 4½ miles

contours are given in metres
The vertical interval is 5m

The wide beach at Holywell Bay is backed by large sand dunes. In summer it is full of people, as is Holywell's medieval pub, The Treguth.

Pilchards

Pilchards used to reach Land's End in enormous shoals in July, and then split so that some travelled along the north coast and some along the south coast of Cornwall. For about four months the huer, whose job it was to spot the shoal, kept a lookout from the cliff top for the silvery-red roughening of the sea and the diving seabirds. When he spotted this he would shout 'hevva', meaning a shoal, down a long tin trumpet to the fishermen at sea, and by an elaborate system of semaphore would direct the boats to shoot the nets around the shoal, which was then towed inshore and the nets anchored. The next process was to 'tuck', or empty, the net. The fish were removed as needed to keep pace with the processing on shore in the pilchard palace. Here the fish were stacked between layers of salt to a height of about five feet and left for a month. Then the fish were packed in barrels with a weight on top to squeeze out the oil – this was sold separately. The cured fish were usually sold to Spain, France and Italy, so giving rise to the expression 'meat, money and light, all in one night'.

Pilchard businesses were sold as 'seines', usually consisting of three boats, two nets and the fish cellars. Some idea of the scale of the industry can be gained from the fact that in 1870 there were 379 registered seines, 285 in St Ives alone, so each seine was allocated a time when it could net the fish. By 1920 the inshore pilchard fishery that had existed for centuries was dead.

Cornish fishermen had never chased just the pilchards, but had a year's work fishing for mackerel from Eddystone to the Wolf Rock from January to June, with herring in the North and Irish Seas being the quarry until the pilchard season started.

In the late twentieth century the pilchard fishery had a small renaissance. Pilchards are just more mature sardines, which many enjoy barbecued on beaches in southern Europe on their holidays, so pilchards are appearing on barbecue menus in Cornwall too. Another new guise for the smaller fish is as a premium product, in oil in bottles or tins, the latter decorated by reproductions of work of the Newlyn School of artists.

But in no way is the fishery approaching the scale of former times, which you can find out about in St Ives Museum. The fish cellars – the 'pilchard palaces' (Cornish *palas*) – are long converted into cafés, or accommodation, or in ruins and robbed for their stone.

3 Newquay to Perranporth

across the Gannel and past Penhale Camp
12.6 miles (20.2 km)

The route to Perranporth is relatively easy, but includes crossing the River Gannel, and some distance along Perran Beach.

From Newquay harbour **21** the Coast Path is waymarked up the steps from the north side of the quay, past the whitewashed Huer's Hut **22** (see page 39) and round a prominent hotel on Towan Head to Fistral Beach, well known to surfers.

To cross the Gannel there are four possible bridges, and one ferry (see page 138), but your choice will be restricted by the time of day, the month, the state of the tide, the weather and sea conditions. At the south end of Fistral Beach **A**, the recommended route takes you left, east, along Pentire Road then down Pentire Crescent, along Penmere Drive and Trevean Way and across the green to the Gannel. Here you can cross the tidal bridge **B** to the mouth of Penpol Creek **C**.

If you cannot cross here, walk upstream between the houses and the river to the next tidal bridge **D**, just before Trenance boating lake. This bridge is higher; remember you have to cross the low-lying salt marsh beyond to reach the route up to Trevemper (a permissive path along the edge of the estuary back to the mouth of Penpol Creek **C** may be available). If bridge **D** is not usable you will need to continue along Gannel Road and the A3075 to Trevemper Bridge **E**, then back through Trevemper, Treringey and Little Trevithick to Penpol Creek **C**.

The final option is to use the private tidal bridge or the ferry at Fern Pit **F**. To reach this you turn right, west, at the south end of Fistral Beach **A**, down Esplanade Road and Riverside Crescent to Fern Pit Café, where, if the café is open, you can walk down through the café's garden and cross the river either by the tidal bridge or by ferry. However you cross the Gannel you should make your way to Rushey Green car park **G**.

(If you are walking in the opposite direction and you wish to use the Fern Pit ferry or bridge **F**, walk to the bottom of the Rushey Green car park **G** and go between the sand dunes and the cliffs. If you wish to use another crossing, leave the car park about one-third of the way down and walk along the path to Penpol **C**. If you cannot cross from there, or by Trenance **D**, you will need to walk up the track to Trevemper Bridge **E**.)

If you want to visit Crantock village, just off the path, you could walk up the lane from Rushey Green car park **G**, but a better car-free route is the path **H** from the western edge of Rushey Green.

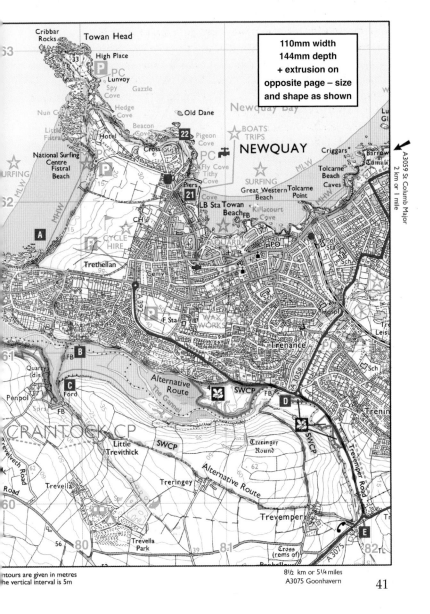

Rushey Green is a mass of tracks but a single path takes you along the edge of the fields, round Pentire Point West into Porth Joke, a sheltered cove sometimes containing a lagoon, where you may see herons. Locally it is known as Polly Joke. Depending on the tides you can miss Holywell by fording the stream at the landward end of the cliffs and taking the stile **I** into Penhale Camp.

From Holywell, known for its holy wells and also its ancient thatched pub, The Treguth, the path skirts the seaward edge of Penhale Camp and then follows Perran Beach to Perranporth.

Prominent red signs emphasise the lack of facilities between Holywell and Perranporth and also the need to keep to the path, avoid short cuts, and obey sentries on the rifle range. The path around the camp is marked by red-and-white-striped posts, which, as far as possible, should be on your landward side. The cliff castle **23** on Penhale Point consists of two impressive ramparts across a steep slope. The rusty-looking Perran Iron Lode shows up at the back of the old quarry **24** below the path at the north end of the beach. There is a waymarked path at the seaward edge of the dunes, or you can walk along the beach if the tide is out. Penhale Sands are Ministry of Defence

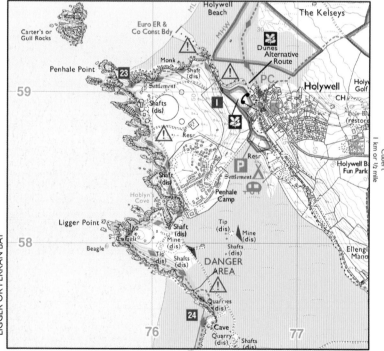

Contours are given in metres
The vertical interval is 5m

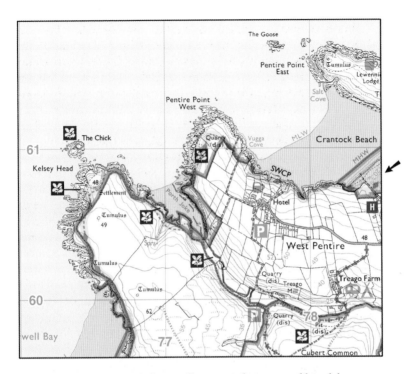

Walkers in springtime can enjoy cowslips among the grass on old sand dunes.

property and out of bounds. The ruined 12th-century St Piran's Church **25**, site of the Domesday monastery of Lanpiran, can be visited, but St Piran's Oratory, probably the oldest church in Cornwall, was in a poor, usually flooded state, even within its protecting concrete bunker, and was re-buried but has recently been excavated and restored. The black-and-white flag often seen flying in Cornwall bears the cross of St Piran, who shares with St Petroc and St Michael the role of Cornwall's patron saint.

At low water you can walk all the way to Perranporth along the beach, possibly admiring the sand yachts, but at high water the sea reaches the foot of the cliffs at Cotty's Point, and you need to walk through the sand dunes, bearing right between the cliffs and the holiday centre and golf links. If you are heading south, the last safe exit from the beach is by concrete steps **J** just south of the adit (a sloping tunnel providing drainage from a mine), with more concrete steps **K** taking the footpath down to the beach south of Cotty's Point and into Perranporth. (If you are heading north, you will find the steps **K** down to the beach located at the seaward end of the fenced path that comes from the holiday camp.) The path continues through the dunes, turning seawards down a 'valley' between sand dunes. In Perranporth there is a large car park at the back of the beach. The youth hostel is the single-storey ex-Admiralty building on Droskyn Point, while the more imposingly military building nearby is a block of flats, recently known as Droskyn Castle Hotel.

JUST OFF THE PATH: *Crantock*

Crantock was the site of the monastery of Langorroc mentioned in Domesday. The rather odd appearance of the church, which was ornately restored at the turn of the century, bears witness to its dual use by monks and lay people. The stocks now in the churchyard were last used about 1817, when they were in the church tower, but you may prefer to rest your legs in The Old Albion pub close by.

Residents of Crantock are very aware that their village has had a far longer and more glorious history than Newquay, which did not start to grow until the railway brought the tourists. Trading vessels came into Porth, to the north of Newquay, or up the Gannel to the south. Among the products exported from the Gannel were lead ingots from the smelter up the valley: the waste was dumped in the estuary.

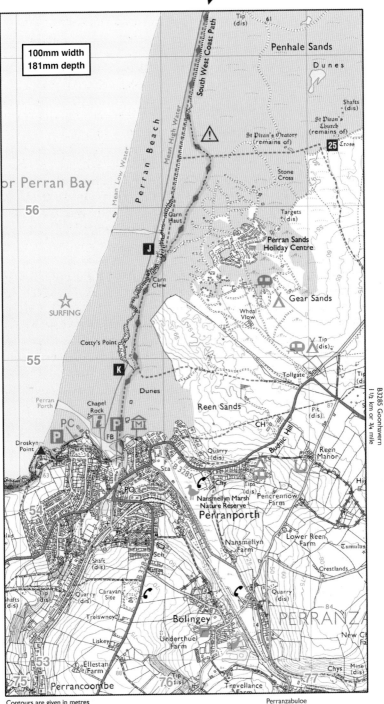

100mm width
181mm depth

Penhale Sands

Dunes

Tip (dis)   61

Shafts (dis)

St Piran's Church (remains of)

South West Coast Path

St Piran's Oratory (remains of)

25 Cross

Perran Beach

Mean High Water

Mean Low Water

or Perran Bay

56

Carn Haut

Stone Cross

J

Carn Clew

Perran Sands Holiday Centre

Targets (dis)

Gear Sands

Wheal Vlow

SURFING

Cotty's Point

Tip (dis)

55

Tollgate

Tip (dis)

K

Dunes

Reen Sands

Perran Porth

Chapel Rock

PC   i

P

M

FB

Droskyn Point

CH

Budnic Hill

Pit (dis)

Reen Manor

PO

F Sta

B3285

Chy

Tips (dis)

Quarry (dis)

Nansmellyn Marsh Nature Reserve

Pencrennow Farm

Perranporth

Lower Reen Farm

Nansmellyn Farm

Tumulus

Shaft (dis)

Sch

Crestlands

Caravan Site

Quarry (dis)

Quarry (dis)

Trelawney

Bolingey

84

PERRANZA

New C Fa

hafts (dis)

Tip (dis)

Underthuel Farm

Liskey

Mine (dis)

Chys

Ellestan Farm

75

Perrancoombe

76

Trevellance Farm

77

Perranzabuloe

B3285 Goonhavern
1½ km or ¾ mile

Contours are given in metres
The vertical interval is 5m

From the mine workings in the foreground to St Agnes Beacon in the distance you walk ove

1 history of wartime airfield, explosives factory, fishing, wrecks, shipbuilding, and much more.

4 Perranporth to Portreath

past St Agnes and Porthtowan
12.4 miles (19.9 km)

This is an easy walk following well-used paths across the flat top of the cliffs, with occasional valleys to cross. You are never very far from the road, a pub, public conveniences and shops.

From Perranporth, the Coast Path follows the hill up Cliff Road, then goes behind the castellated apartments and the youth hostel and on to the cliff top. (If you are heading north and looking for the hostel, you should find a sign where the hostel path branches off to the left.)

The coast from Perranporth to Porthtowan has as much evidence of mining as anywhere in Cornwall, although currently the area around Levant, Geevor and Botallack has more in the way of interpretation for the visitor. Much of the evidence here has been destroyed by the elements or by man. For example, if

Contours are given in metres
The vertical interval is 5m

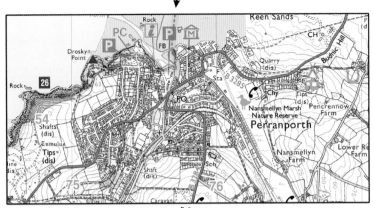

Contours are given in metres
The vertical interval is 5m

Bolingey

you look east from the track **26** near Shag Rock, the old men's workings can be seen riddling the slate cliffs. The area around Cligga Head draws people with many interests: geologists, mineral-hunters, rock-climbers, and glider pilots, whose club house **27** is part of the buildings of the old British and Colonial Explosives factory. The airfield dates from the Second World War and is little changed, but the relics of the explosives factory and of the processing works for the tin mines are far less easy to disentangle. Cligga Mine yielded tungsten as well as tin and, like many tungsten producers, was worked in the last world war to supply tungsten for armour-plating and armour-piercing shells. In the early 1980s the mine was sampled again, but the programme stopped when the price of tin dropped from more than £10,000 per tonne to less than £4,000 in 1985.

Hanover Cove **28** is named after the Falmouth packet boat that was carrying gold coins valued at £60,000 when she was wrecked here in 1763. Above the cove you may be able to find a large granite boundstone marking the edge of a 'sett', an area of ground granted to a group of men willing to prospect for ore.

Bats, including the rare Greater Horseshoe, live inside the disused mines, and conical mesh caps ('bat castles') have been put over old shafts to make them safe, but still allow the bats access. Please do not drop stones into the shafts to see how deep they are.

When you reach Trevellas 'porth' or cove **29**, look up the valley, which still has evidence of mining and tin smelting from medieval times to the present. The path follows the east side of the valley before crossing the bridge by the Blue Hills engine house, and the entrance to Blue Hills tin streams **30**, and then you are on the track used every Easter for the London to Land's End motor trials. If you want to understand how Cornishmen, women and boys worked tin you can do no better than visit the tin streams before continuing. The Wills family won, processed and smelted tin here long before the operation was opened to visitors. The Wills also help to support Prince Charles as they pay royalties on each tonne of tin produced to the Duchy of Cornwall (page 120).

Above Trevaunance Cove, the Coronation Walk leaves the path at **A** and takes you into St Agnes, a pleasant village just off the path (page 53) with a museum in the former chapel of rest **31**.

Trevaunance Cove used to have St Agnes harbour on its west side. Here coal was raised by a horse-powered whim, and ore went down a chute from the ore-bins **32**, which are still visible. An unrepaired gap in the breakwater in 1915 resulted in the harbour becoming a mass of scattered granite blocks on the sea bed. You will find a good range of facilities, including buses, in St Agnes village. The pub, The Driftwood Spars, has photographs of the harbour and local wrecks, and also brews its own beer.

From the pub in Trevaunance Cove you start to climb up the valley-side by the steep lane opposite, but then you take the little track behind the block of flats and will find yourself back on a lane above the cove; the open cliff top is not far away. Above Polberro Cove was Polberro Mine, famous for the richness of its tin ore.

Offshore, Bawden Rocks, or Man and his man, have a bird colony that includes guillemots, razorbills and black-backed gulls. Puffins have been seen, and may still breed here. Around Newdowns Head **33** grey seals breed in the caves: the pups are born in November or early December.

St Agnes now has a Voluntary Marine Conservation Area in recognition of the diversity of its marine life. The designated area is a breeding ground for fish, so conserving it should help the local fishermen have a sustainable future.

The cliff top on both sides of the old coastguard station **34** is a favoured spot for hang-gliders and flyers of radio-controlled model gliders, because of the up-draughts from the cliffs produced by any wind between north and north-west.

On the rocks around the National Trust-owned St Agnes Beacon there are some geologically very young sands and clays (less than 50 million years old). The sand has been worked for centuries and is mostly used for making moulds. Large quantities went from Doble's Pit **35**, and other quarries, to the foundries, such as those at Hayle (page 64). Clay from St Agnes was puddled (walked all over when wet) to make a waterproof base when

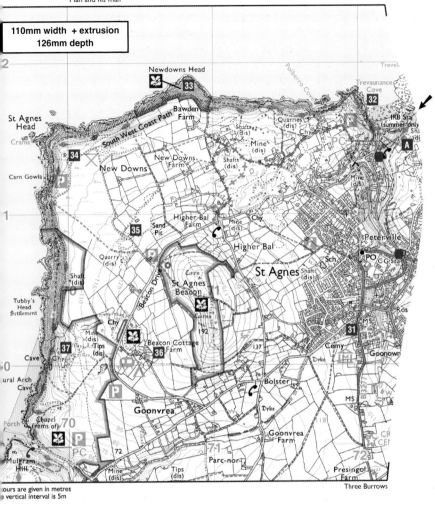

110mm width + extrusion
126mm depth

the piers were being built in Penzance harbour. However, clay
was mostly used to attach candles to miners' felt hats, or to rock,
when working underground – the pits **36** behind Beacon Cottage
Farm supplied this. Bernard Leach, who made many of his pots
in St Ives, also used clay from St Agnes.

To the west are the much photographed remains of Wheal
Coates **37**, with the clifftop view now accessible to wheelchair
users. If you walk back up the beach at low tide from Chapel
Porth, with its public conveniences and excellent café (try a
'hedgehog'!), you can see in the cliffs an adit and one of the
lodes that was worked by this mine.

51

South of Porthtowan, site of a short-lived smelter, the path is kept away from crumbling cliffs, following the perimeter fence of Nancekuke, which has been both an RAF airfield and a chemical warfare base. The steps down Sally's Bottom are made of distinctive Portuguese granite, quite different from the local granite.

Portreath harbour **38** was once known as Basset's Cove, because the lords of the manor, the Bassets of Tehidy, used it for recreation, and as well as installing their bathing machine and a cottage they also cut six baths in the rock for sea-water bathing.

A daymark – 'The Pepperpot' – sits above the harbour, which was built by the Bassets in stages from 1760 after the original harbour on the west side of the bay was destroyed. Wagons loaded with ore would have been run down the incline **39**, built in 1838 as part of the Hayle Railway, to the harbour. From Portreath you can walk across Cornwall to Devoran on the 11 mile (17.5km) Coast-to-Coast Trail: this also has links to many World Heritage sites.

Portreath has a good range of shops, cafés, a post office, accommodation, and buses both to Camborne and Redruth. Inland at Nance Farm is a YHA bunkhouse, best reached by a short walk through Illogan Woods.

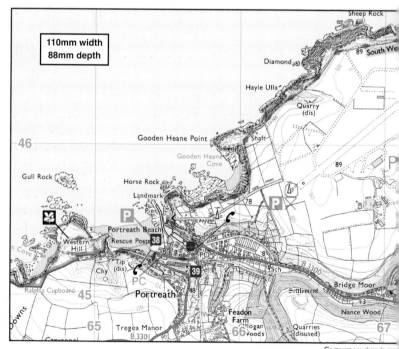

Contours are given in me
The vertical interval is 5

ntours are given in metres
he vertical interval is 5m

3¾ km or 2¼ miles
Bridge

JUST OFF THE PATH: *St Agnes*

In a county where tourism is of great economic importance, it is refreshing that St Agnes has butchers and bakers rather than shops selling mementos to tourists. Even the Tourist Information Centre (TIC) is just part of the video and DVD hire shop, which of course keeps far longer hours than a normal TIC! The best route to the village from the Coast Path is along the Coronation Walk, above Trevaunance Cove. This takes you straight into Peterville, where you will find a 21st-century mermaid on The Peterville Inn's sign. Beyond Stippy Stappy, a stepped terrace of houses built for sea captains, is the church and village centre, with TIC. Further on, in the cemetery among former butchers, bakers, miners and seamen (though not the ones successfully enticed by earlier mermaids, who needed no silicone enhancement), the former chapel of rest **31** contains St Agnes Museum – 'from fishing to folklore, tin mining to turtles'; entrance is free.

Cornish mining

Metal has been coming out of Cornwall for thousands of years. But the question of how the metal got there in the first place goes back over millions of years. Apart from the gold, of which there is only a small amount, the metals are locked up in minerals as oxides or sulphides, or more complex compounds, so that what men mined were ores of the metals which then had to be processed and smelted. Most of the ore was formed as a result of the intrusions of granitic magma from deep within the earth's crust between 290 and 270 million years ago. These set up convection cells in the water present in the surrounding muddy rocks, which also contained tiny amounts of metals. The flowing hot water dissolved these metals, which later crystallised out in veins as the water cooled at the top of the granite or in the rocks above. As Cornish granites contain a significant amount of uranium and this slowly decays, releasing heat, the convection has continued, and ore veins ('lodes') often show a very complex sequence of events. Broadly there are two sets of lodes, the earlier set carries mostly tin and copper, while later ones carry lead, silver, zinc and iron, and often run north–south. The early lodes usually run north-east–south-west (except in the Land's End area) and you can see this pattern in the lines of the engine houses.

Similar processes involving flowing hot water, plus some later weathering, also converted much of the feldspar in the granite into china clay, or kaolin, and this has been more valuable to Cornwall's economy than all the metals. From the Coast Path around Newquay you can see the vast waste tips for the clay pits north of St Austell.

Men started exploiting the tin ores in the Bronze Age, working the sediments in valley bottoms after erosion had stripped off the overlying rock and then worn away the exposed lode. Rocks and grains containing tin minerals were more dense than granite and quartz so were left behind by the flowing water and became concentrated. Over time underground mining developed, but the main problem was water and various technologies were developed to remove this. Mines close to the sea or river valleys were drained by gently sloping tunnels, 'adits', but there was a lower limit to mines drained in this way. Nevertheless, extensive systems of adits were built, stretching for several miles. The development of steam-powered pumps by Newcomen, and later by Boulton and Watt, meant miners could work deeper. But their engines worked close to atmospheric pressure: locally Richard Trevithick developed engines using 'strong steam', at 65 pounds per square inch above atmospheric. Foundries such as Harvey's of Hayle developed bigger and more powerful engines to pump the water out of mines, wind up the ore and power stamps to crush the rock. New developments also took place in mineral processing and smelting, and large parts of Cornwall in the 19th century were industrialised. The centre of the mining was in Camborne and Redruth, and there is still much to see in that area, including two engines owned by the NT. Mining schools also developed, the most famous being Camborne School of Mines (CSM). In 2006 UNESCO designated the Cornish Mining Landscape a World Heritage Site.

The price of copper crashed in the 1870s, followed by tin in the 1890s, and that basically spelled the end of Cornish mining. If you want to find out more about Cornish mining, CSM has a virtual museum at www.ex.ac.uk/geomincentre A superb collection of Cornish minerals, the Rashleigh Collection, is in the Royal Cornwall Mueum in Truro, where you can also see many exhibits about mining and archaeology.

From The Crowns, an inclined shaft went under the sea. Miners could hear boulders rolling about above their heads during storms.

5 Portreath to St Ives

via Gwithian and Lelant
17.9 miles (28.7 km)

This is almost all easy walking, but includes walking beside the main road around Hayle harbour. From the large car park above Portreath beach follow the main road across the bridge, then go up Battery Hill. Before the continuation of the Battery Hill road **40** dives back to the beach, there is a narrow track to the south of Western Hill. To get a good view of Portreath and its difficult harbour, climb up Western Hill, which is owned by the National Trust, as is much of the coast as far as Gwithian. The road often lies close to the coast and the Trust has improved many of the areas where cars can be parked, making access easy for people who wish to walk only a short distance.

(As a contrast to the Coast Path, or if the weather is poor at the coast, there is a range of marked trails in Tehidy Country Park. The Park is owned by Cornwall County Council and managed by its countryside rangers. The quickest route is to leave the coast **A** just south of Basset's Cove: you can return by the path at **B**.)

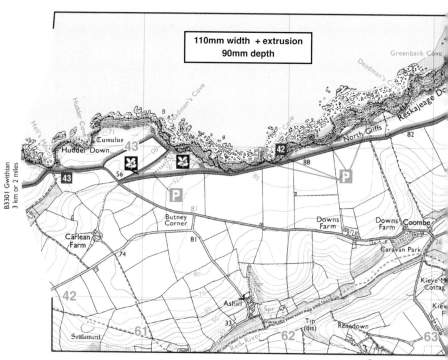

Contours are given in metre
The vertical interval is 5m

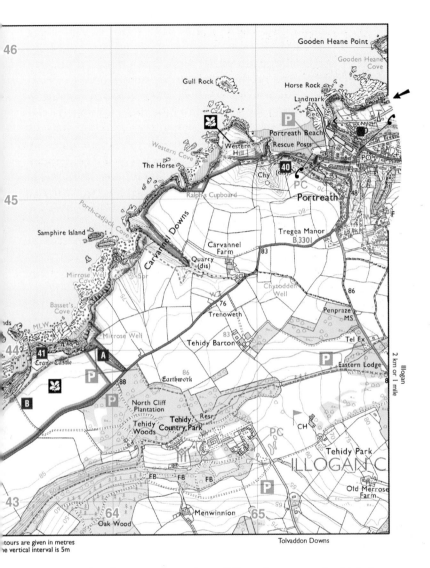

tours are given in metres
the vertical interval is 5m

Crane Castle **41**, an Iron Age cliff castle, most of which has been eroded by the sea over the last 2,000 years, seems to be oddly named, but it is thought originally to have been called *'ker hen'* or 'old fort'. At the east end of Derrick Cove the National Trust has made a cliff viewing platform **42** for visitors in wheelchairs. Hell's Mouth **43** is a local tourist site, where a very short walk from the road takes the less energetic to the top of a spectacular drop to the beach, then back to the café, with water from a private borehole for the tea.

Look out for grey seals as you walk out towards Navax Point **44**. They use the caves below as breeding sites, and from October to April large numbers congregate. Over 70 have been counted hauled out on the beach at one time. Godrevy Island **45**, with its lighthouse, the inspiration for Virginia Woolf's *To the Lighthouse*, marks the landward end of a treacherous line of reefs, The Stones, which have claimed many wrecks. Perhaps the best known involved the loss of some of King Charles I's personal effects in 1646. His wife and his son, who became King Charles II at the Restoration, had fled separately to France via Pendennis Castle at Falmouth, which was then a royalist stronghold. The goods that came ashore were fought over on the beach by Bassets and Arundells, each claiming wrecking rights as lords of the manor. Apparently, although the goods landed within the Bassets' territory they did not press their case, as they had supported the royalist cause, which by then was all but lost, even in Cornwall.

Just before you cross the Red River **46** by footbridge there is a NT café in an award-winning modern building. This is open in the season and weekends and holidays all year.

The Red River once discharged thousands of tons a day of red iron oxide, residue from the tin mines, in its lifeless waters. The water also carried fine-grained cassiterite, lost from the mines' processing operations, and some of this was recovered by a series of tin-streaming works in the Red River valley. Much of the cassiterite reached the sea and was deposited on the sea bed, so that whenever the price of tin was high, plans were made to dredge it from the sea bed. Places like St Ives, which rely on tourists enjoying sandy beaches, objected that the waste dumped back in the sea might pollute the beaches.

The beach at Gwithian is good for surfing and the area is full of chalets and holiday camps. A route has been waymarked through the '*towans*' (Cornish for sand dunes), but you may prefer to walk along the beach if the tide is out. In summer you may have to pick your way through sunbathing bodies – the dune route will be easier.

The banks and bunkers among the dunes were part of an explosives factory, once one of the largest in Britain, employing over 1,800 people; locally this area is called Dynamite Towans **47**. Nowadays the dunes are better known for their diverse habitats and wildlife – 300 species of plant have been recorded, as well as many butterflies and moths, and glow-worms. Dunes are dynamic, but they suffer from excessive trampling in

45

Godrevy Island
(WITHIAN CP)

Godrevy
Point

44

Nathaga
Rocks

Navax Point

Mutton
Cove

Kynance Cove

The Knavocks

76

Tumulus

SWC Path

P
PC

The Cleaders

Godrevy Farm

Homestead

Godrevy Rocks

Godrevy Cove

Manor House
(remains of)

Higher Pencobben

MS

Castle Giver Cove

Fishing Cove

73

67

P

43

B3301 Portreath
8 km or 5 miles

Magow Rocks

46

P

Godrevy Towans

Sand
Cot

Settlements

Mean Low Water

Mean High Water

Gwithian Bridge

6

42

Gillick Rock

St Gotbian's Chapel

Reskajeage

ck Rock

Garrack

Co Const Bdy

Quarry
(dis)

Strap Rocks

Alternative Route

St Churchtown Road

12

es Rock

Green Lane

PC

Nanterrow
Farm

P

Gwithian
Towans

Cross

P

Shaft

Gwithian
21

Quarry
(dis)

Peter's Point

Settlement

Quarry
(dis)

41

⚠

Calize

Engew
Farm

32

Godrevy
Cottage

Pennance

Nanterrow
Cottage

P

St Ives Lane

59

Prosper Hill

Pennance Vean

Shaft

47

Lissadel

69

57

Trevarnon
Round

78

Upton Towans

Adit

Trevarnon
Farm

Gwithian Road

Works

Earthwork

Cemetery

Chy
Shaft

Treeve Farm

58

Pulsack Manor

59

Trevarnon Moor

Connerto

ntours are given in metres
he vertical interval is 5m

summer and gales in winter, so major conservation work is being undertaken on many of Cornwall's dune systems to preserve these habitats.

If you walked along the beach, you need to leave it beyond the lifeguard's hut **C**, which is just to the east of where the rocky cliff starts again. The track then winds among chalets, passing spiny sea buckthorn bushes, until a car park is reached at the mouth of the Hayle Estuary. Some of the banks on the Lelant side have been strengthened by a ship-breaker, with parts of a First World War destroyer. A ferry no longer makes the short crossing, but it is possible that the service will be reinstated. Without a ferry you have to walk to the old swing bridge **D** and then around Hayle harbour by road if you wish to continue to St Ives.

If you want to continue walking, turn east from the 100-year-old swing bridge **D** at the entrance to Hayle harbour. This is the oldest swing bridge with its machinery left in Britain, and

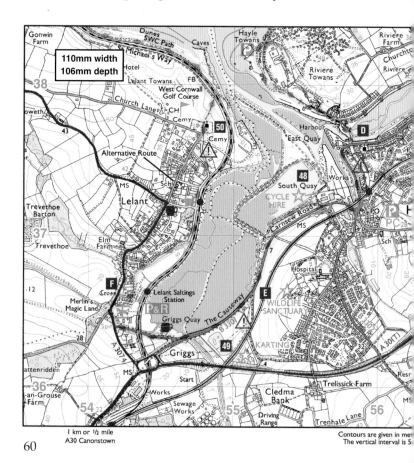

1 km or ½ mile
A30 Canonstown

Contours are given in metres
The vertical interval is 5

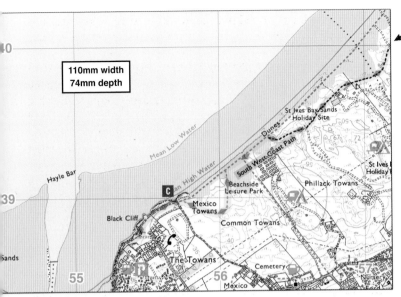

Contours are given in metres
The vertical interval is 5m

is very wide, having been built for the Great Western Railway's broad gauge. Follow the road along the inlet, under the viaduct and into Foundry Square, then under the viaduct again. The path is routed around Carnsew Pool **48**, which is a good place from which to view the centre of the estuary. The RSPB owns the intertidal mudflats of the whole estuary. Over 270 species of bird have been recorded in the Hayle Estuary and some species, such as wigeon, teal and curlew, sometimes overwinter in significant numbers. Of course, when twitchers' pagers announce the arrival of an extreme rarity, you are liable to see flocks of birdwatchers from all over the UK all looking at one tired and hungry American vagrant. In the old days such an exotic visitor would have been shot and stuffed.

A short walk up the lane **E** will bring you to the RSPB hide above the scrapes at Ryan's Field **49**. Inside is information about what has been seen recently in west Cornwall, as well as identification charts for the non-experts.

Following the road further round the estuary, turn right on to The Saltings, the minor road where a cross is built into the hedge **F**. This drops down to the shore and the railway line and then rejoins the main road just before the church **50**. Alternatively you can keep to the main road between **F** and **50**, passing The Badger Inn. St Michael's Way, a 12-mile (19.5-km) footpath to St Michael's Mount, starts here. There are two slate memorials

Pink thrift clothes the slopes around the spectacular chasm of Hell's Mouth, east of Godrevy.

inside the church and four old granite crosses in the churchyard. The bank round the churchyard is made of slag from the Copperhouse smelter. The cemetery on your left is a wonderful mass of wild flowers, truly a 'living churchyard'.

The Coast Path now crosses the golf course, then passes under the railway bridge and along the dunes behind Port Kidney Sands.

The path is well marked into St Ives, but you can take a short diversion to St Uny's Well **51**.

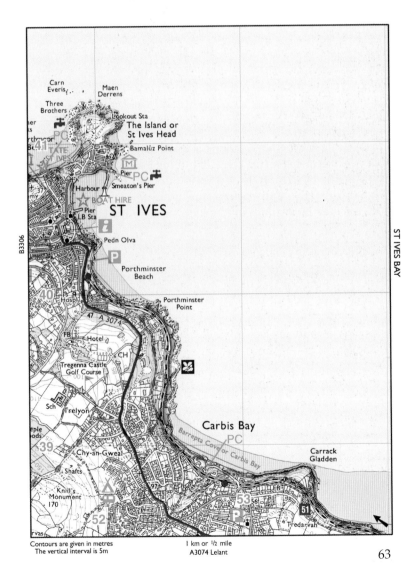

Contours are given in metres
The vertical interval is 5m

1 km or ½ mile
A3074 Lelant

St Ives

Nowadays St Ives is famous as a tourist resort and for the Tate Gallery St Ives, which devotes some of its space to the work of the exceptional group of artists who came to work in the area. Names that are associated with St Ives include the potter Bernard Leach, the sculptor Barbara Hepworth and the painters Ben Nicholson, Roger Hilton, Peter Lanyon, Terry Frost and Patrick Heron, as well as the primitive painter Alfred Wallis. Work by Barbara Hepworth and others is scattered through the town: outside the TIC, in the library and church; and her studio and garden are open as an outpost of the Tate, so you can enjoy looking at semi-tropical vegetation through one of her pierced forms (or vice versa). The Tate sells a leaflet, *Stones of Land and Sea*, for the Hepworth sculpture trail. Many people leave St Ives with a turquoise seascape – there appears to be several production lines! – but there is more challenging work available too.

St Ives achieved earlier fame as the most important port for the pilchard fishery (see page 39), with its harbour, protected by Smeaton's Pier, full of boats and the town reeking of pilchards. Many objects from this industry, as well as much else, are kept in the museum, which is well worth a visit.

Harvey's of Hayle, and Richard Trevithick

Hayle used to consist of two quite separate industrial communities, Hayle to the west and Copperhouse to the east, whose intense rivalry as providers of machinery and materials for the mines led to violent intervention in each other's operations. Copperhouse was the scene of a short-lived attempt to smelt copper ore in Cornwall rather than taking the ore to the coal in the Swansea valley. Hayle was better known for its foundries, with Harvey's being not only pre-eminent but also the longest survivor. Harvey's made engines for metal and coal mines, for moving sewage (for example, one of the Kew Bridge Engines in London), and for pumping water in Holland. It also built iron ships and the iron work for the Royal Albert Bridge across the Tamar, which Isambard Kingdom Brunel built in 1859, and over which all the trains to and from Cornwall still travel. Harvey's engines could be found almost everywhere in the world to which Cornish men had taken their skills in hard-rock mining, and one is preserved locally at Levant Mine.

Associated with Harvey's were some notable engineers, of whom only Richard Trevithick (1771–1833) has received much acknowledgement. Trevithick, and others, advocated the use of high-pressure steam, at 65 pounds per square inch (psi) or more, rather than at only 2–3 psi, as in the Newcomen and Watt engines then in use. Trevithick also designed steam-powered vehicles, building the world's first passenger-carrying self-propelled car in 1801 (Cugnot had build a machine to tow artillery around Paris 30 years earlier). In 1804 he built the world's first locomotive, for the Penydarren ironworks in Wales, several decades before Stephenson's *Rocket*. To celebrate the bicentenary, The Trevithick Society made a steam-worked replica of Trevithick's road vehicle, and on Christmas Eve 2001 it was indeed 'Goin' up Camborne 'ill comin' down', as the local song has it. A steam-worked replica of the locomotive can be seen in the Welsh Industrial and Maritime Museum in Cardiff.

Inside the smaller of these engine houses at Levant, a Cornish engine, originally built by Harvey's in 1840, can be seen steaming.

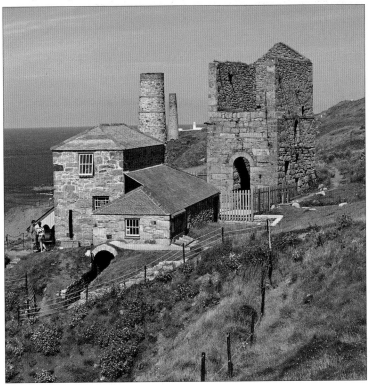

6 St Ives to Zennor

via Clodgy Point
6.5 miles (10.4 km)

This is a short but testing stretch, and half a day allows you plenty of time with St Ia's town, St Ives, at one end and the Mermaid of Zennor at the other. Since there is no accommodation, shops, pubs or cafés on the path between St Ives and Sennen, a distance of about 20 miles (32 km), it makes sense to book accommodation ahead at one of the villages off the path, and Zennor has much to recommend it.

From the harbour at St Ives you can cut through to Porthmeor beach and pick up the path on Beach Road. However, the official route goes past Smeaton's Pier **52** and to the museum, and then round The Island, which is said to be the best place in Britain to watch the migration of seabirds. On the hilltop is a chapel dedicated to St Nicholas **53**, the patron saint of seafarers. This probably exhibited a light to guide fishermen before lighthouses were built. At the back of Porthmeor beach is the Tate Gallery **54**, on the site of the old gasworks. The building, by Evans and Shalev, has won awards and even if you do not want to view the pictures and the pottery, you can get a free pass to walk past the stained-glass window by Patrick Heron and upstairs to the bookshop and

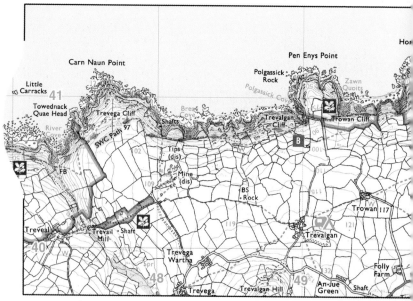

66

Contours are given in met
The vertical interval is 5

excellent rooftop café/restaurant. Of course you could pay and see the work of artists who lived in the area and, indeed, how diverse artists have seen the area through which you are walking.

Once on Beach Road, a waymark by the bowling green **A** shows that you are on the Coast Path, which is an easy walk as far as Clodgy Point (*clodgy* is Cornish for leper). From Clodgy Point all the way to Cape Cornwall the coastal strip is a Site of Special Scientific Interest (SSSI), and some is defined as an Environmentally Sensitive Area (ESA), see page 71. Roughly half of this coast is protected by the National Trust, including Hellesveor Cliff and Hor Point. The going is rough, as the track is uneven and boggy in places, although stepping stones and even a piece of boardwalk at Trevalgan Cliff **B** make for drier feet. There is a plethora of information signs here, and a very modern circle of stones, all related to the campsite inland but rather out of keeping with the wildness of the coast. The Coast Path carries straight on, while a much-used path bears uphill, and left, to the campsite. The bogginess brings its own flora, including refreshing mint to chew and orchids to look at. Some streams have royal fern and you may find Cornish moneywort and pale butterwort. Near Polgassick Cove a badger sett and the path coincide, and it is common to see seals 'bottling' or hauled out on rocks: The Carracks are a favourite spot.

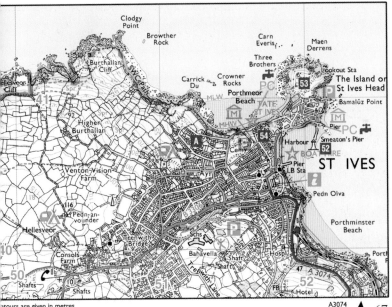

There are a few mining relics and hundreds of little fields with the stones cleared to form boundaries. The fields date from the Bronze or Iron Ages and most are still being farmed. People tried to get food from the sea here, too, and boats were launched from Wicca Pool **55** and Porthzennor Cove **56**.

If you are intending to stop at Zennor (see page 70), leave the Coast Path at a junction **C** on the west side of Zennor Head, and follow the track to the village.

Many people spend half a day walking to Zennor along the Coast Path from St Ives, then return by a far easier route along the Zennor church path across the fields. This path leaves Zennor between the churchyard and the village hall and links the hamlets of Tremedda, Tregerthen, Wicca, Trevega, Trevalgan and Trowan. Returning by the open-topped bus to St Ives in summertime is an option taken by some who have been surprised by the strenuousness of the Coast Path.

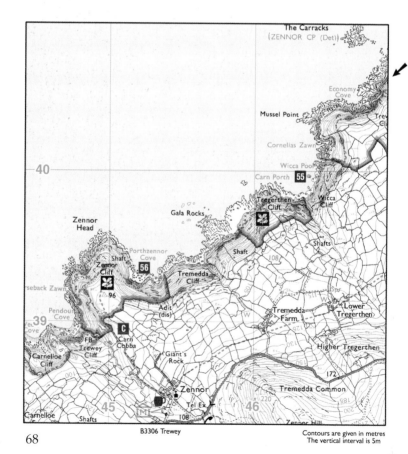

B3306 Trewey

Contours are given in metres
The vertical interval is 5m

Out of season you may have the tough but rewarding section between St Ives and Zennor to yourself.

69

JUST OFF THE PATH: *Zennor*

Zennor is a good place to get off the Coast Path for a few hours, or overnight. It has no shops, but it does have a good pub and places to stay, and a public telephone and buses to St Ives, St Just, Land's End and Penzance. The reasons to visit Zennor are conveniently in a line. First is the church with the famous mermaid carved on a bench end. She is a traditional maid, holding a comb and a mirror. Beneath the tower is a slate gravestone for a young man killed in a mining accident – there are many such in Cornwall. Outside, on the wall, is a memorial to John Davey, who died in 1891 and is reputed to have been the last person with some traditional knowledge of Cornish. Next door to the church is The Tinner's Arms, where you can wash down your food with a pint of Mermaid! In summer cream teas are also popular. A few yards away the former chapel has been converted to a backpackers' hostel. The Wayside Museum, across the stream, grew out of one man's private passion in the 1930s to preserve the evidence of the area's vanishing way of life. There are no buttons to press and very little evidence of designers; instead, the 5,000 or so items are mostly left to speak for themselves (though there is a quiz sheet to keep youngsters busy). From the outside the museum looks tiny, but many people spend two hours or more inside.

Zennor is a typical West Cornwall village, but with a mermaid.

Up the hill, and beside the road, is a stone from which John Wesley preached, and beyond are a couple of farms where you are likely to find visitors from all over the world enjoying farmhouse B&B. D. H. Lawrence and his German wife stayed near Zennor during the First World War and experienced rather less hospitality. They left after being accused of leaving curtains undrawn at night to guide German submarines.

Inland from Zennor is Zennor Quoit, a very large neolithic tomb which also seems to have been used in the Bronze Age. Parts of it were again used in the 19th century by the local farmer in making a shed nearby. Fortunately his efforts at recycling were eventually successfully discouraged by the local vicar. Fortunate, too, that the vicar's great-grandfather, Dr William Borlase, had recorded the tomb in an earlier, more complete state.

West Penwith Environmentally Sensitive Area

ESAs are designated to protect traditional farming landscapes at risk. The scheme is managed by Natural England. In the West Penwith ESA farmers are invited to take part in a voluntary scheme and receive a management payment to maintain and enhance the wildlife, landscape and archaeology. Farmers work to a set of stipulations that include maintaining existing field patterns and grazing rough land with cattle. They are eligible for capital payments to rebuild Cornish hedges, restore traditional buildings, protect historic features and restore wildlife habitats such as the Western heath and maritime grassland. The intention is not to create a museum, but to enable farmers to maintain an ancient working landscape. The alternative would be either dereliction and abandonment or amalgamation of tiny fields and loss of rare habitats to make farms suitable for highly mechanised agriculture. In either case, the landscape would change, historic features would be lost and the diversity of wildlife would decrease.

It has been suggested that the field boundaries are the oldest man-made structures in the world still in continuous use, though this is impossible to prove. The dating of these fields as Bronze Age – from the second millennium BC – is by comparison with similar structures on Bodmin Moor which are connected to date-able objects. The project is seen as a success in that around 90 per cent of the eligible area (i.e. 7,800 of 8,600 hectares) is under protective management, representing an uptake of approximately 90% by farmers. In addition, many buildings have been restored and many Cornish hedges rebuilt.

7 Zennor to Cape Cornwall

passing Pendeen Watch and Botallack Head
11.2 miles (18 km)

From the village at Zennor you take the track between the pub and the church and follow it to the west side of Zennor Head to join the Coast Path.

Pendour Cove **57** is also known as Mermaid Cove and, although you are unlikely to hear her singing, in the evening you might hear the badgers snuffling around by the sett beside the path. A little further on you can see the spectacular royal fern, which is nationally rare but occurs fairly commonly in Cornwall. When the Victorian craze for fern gardens was at its height, large numbers were dug up in the wild. Today there are different fads in garden design, but orchids are always vulnerable because of collectors; there are several species along the coast, as well as bog asphodel.

Treen Cove, sheltered from the prevailing south-westerly winds by Gurnard's Head, was the site of both a pilchard seine (see page 39) and a more obvious tin mine above Lean Point. Gurnard's Head is supposed to bear a similarity to the fish,

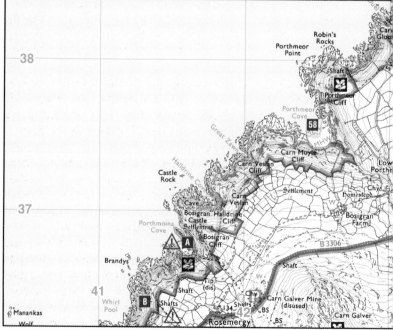

B3306 Trevowhan

Contours are given in met
The vertical interval is 5r

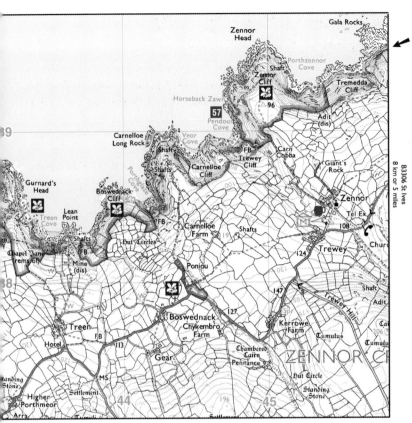

which most think ugly but which has a sculptural beauty, as well as being good stewed in cider or baked in foil. The headland is notable for its cliff castle and the remains of round houses and is now in the ownership of the National Trust (as a surprisingly prominent sign informs everyone).

On the west side of Porthmeor Cove **58** veins of light-coloured granite can be seen to cut through the original darker rock. The granite came in as a liquid several kilometres underground and can be seen only because the rock above has been eroded away over the last 280 million years.

Take care at Bosigran Cliff **A**, as many of the paths joining the Coast Path end at the top of sheer rock faces. These are suitable for either climbing up or abseiling down, and there are climbs here suitable for all levels of competence. If you are walking from the west you can often watch an ascent through binoculars as you approach, but beware of the sloping shaft right by the path **B**.

As you reach Portheras Cove **59** the signs of people not just coexisting with nature but trying to conquer it become stronger. The fields become larger, the houses more obvious, and there is more evidence of tin working. You are advised not to go on to the beach with bare feet because of sharp metal from the *Alacrity*, a coaster wrecked in 1963 and later blown up.

Pendeen House **60** was the birthplace of the great Cornish antiquarian William Borlase, whose comments on Cornwall in the 18th century are often quoted. In the farmyard behind the house is one of the largest fougous in Cornwall. These are underground chambers, but whether they were for storage or for ritual purposes is not known.

Pendeen Lighthouse **61** was opened in 1900 because passing vessels were unable to see either the Longships or Trevose lights. Both could be hidden by high cliffs, and there were many wrecks, particularly on Gurnard's Head and on The Wra. In May 1995 the lighthouse was automated, and the keepers' cottages are now holiday lets. The village of Pendeen,

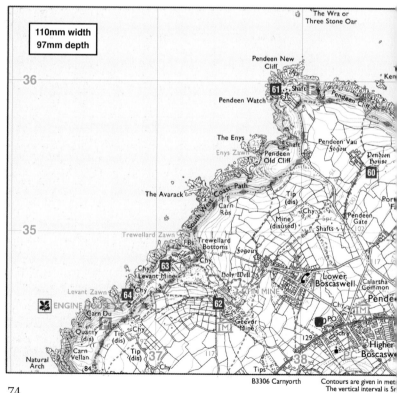

B3306 Carnyorth

Contours are given in met
The vertical interval is 5r

along the road from the lighthouse, should meet most walkers' needs. The population is less than St Just's, inland from Cape Cornwall, but it is larger than any village on the route from St Ives. The reason for the size is Geevor Mine **62**, which took over the workings of the old Levant **63** and Botallack mines. Geevor Mine itself closed in 1990 and the area is no longer prosperous. As in previous closures, many miners have emigrated, but a few retired men have found jobs – as guides at Geevor Tin Mine Heritage Centre, which is open Sunday to Friday all year. Back at the coast the indoor beam engine **64** at Levant Mine has been restored by members of the Trevithick Society and can be seen steaming. The engine was built by Harvey's of Hayle (see page 64) and was last used in 1930. It is the oldest surviving engine in Cornwall and is owned by the National Trust, which chose the coastal strip from Pendeen to Cape Cornwall as its project for 1995, the Trust's Centenary Year. Since then, further grants have funded more restoration, plus the development of a small visitor centre in the Counthouse Workshop, Botallack.

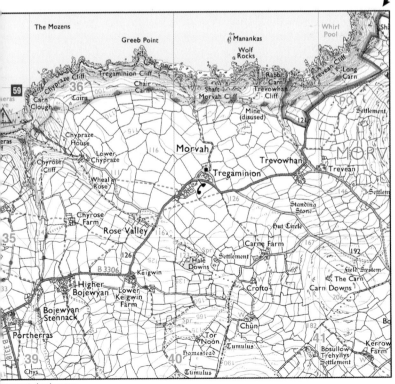

Contours are given in metres
The vertical interval is 5m

Evidence of mining is found everywhere along this coast, but the most photographed relic must be the two engine houses **65** by the inclined Crowns Shaft of Botallack. These were restored by the Carn Brea Mining Society. The workings stretched under the sea, and in Levant Mine not only could the miners hear boulders moving about on the sea bed over their heads, but after the mine closed the sea broke into the workings. The mines produced mainly tin and copper, but also some arsenic, uranium and bismuth. You can learn more at Geevor's Hard Rock Museum and at Botallack Counthouse **66**.

At Kenidjack Castle **67** there is almost a surfeit of history. The engine houses were robbed to make the butts of the rifle range, and from the butts you can look down on a Bronze Age cairn. In the valley below there are the remains of many water-powered stamps for crushing the ores, and a recently restored arsenic calciner.

Cape Cornwall was thought in earlier days to be the most westerly point in England, but now that the crowds go to Land's End, it is relatively peaceful. The place is almost a microcosm of Cornwall, with fishing boats, mining remains, religious ruins and subtropical plants. And a new golf course. In 2000 the NT bought the golf course, and then reduced the input of nitrates so that the course is not now such an alien dark green. The Cape itself was a gift to the Trust from Heinz to celebrate the food company's centenary.

Land's End Youth Hostel is in the Cot Valley, about 1 mile (1.5 km) along the coast from Cape Cornwall, and rather further from Land's End.

If you want to walk to St Just, there are pleasant routes up both the Kenidjack and the Cot valleys – far more appealing than following the road from Cape Cornwall.

JUST OFF THE PATH: *St Just*

St Just has been in existence for hundred of years, with a medieval core of the church, several houses, including The Star, a pub, and an open-air theatre, the Plen-an-Gwarry, which pre-dates Shakespeare's Globe by over a century. St Just's more recent history has been bound up with the fortunes of the local mines, with the planned development of an industrial town in the 19th century as the mines prospered. But in 1900 many of the houses were reported to be derelict,

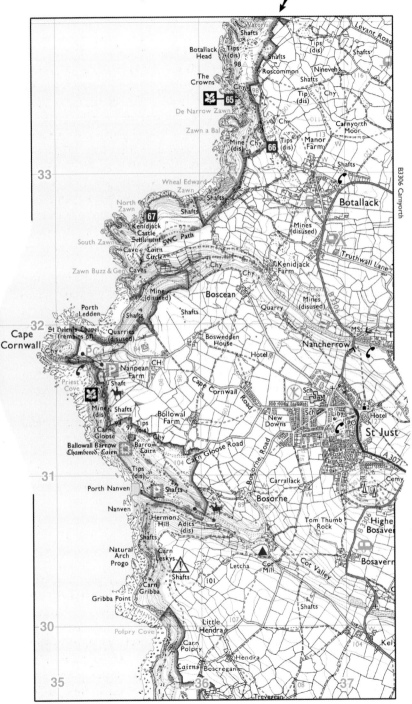

Contours are given in metres
The vertical interval is 5m

77

Cape Cornwall was once thought to be the land's end, the most westerly point. It probably has more to offer the lover of Cornwall than Land's End today.

after the price of tin crashed and miners emigrated. The local economy suffered too when Geevor, the last tin mine in the area, closed in 1990. In 2004 a regeneration project was funded, but the careful plans brought in by the appointed designers caused some debate. Some St Just people did not see that 'Mediterranean-style piazzas' were appropriate to a granite village blasted by gales. The plans included use of granite, locally sourced if possible – and here the locals insisted that the granite was indeed local, or at least Cornish, not Chinese or Portuguese or from anywhere else, and was brownish, not grey, to match the existing buildings.

If you visit St Just you will find a good range of pubs, shops and cafés, as well as two butchers where a notice on the counter will inform you exactly where the steak in your pasty came from (which farm and which breed of cattle). If you visit in the summer you may be fortunate enough to see a Cornish mystery play performed by the local community. These date from the 14th century and are written in Cornish, though the performances are in English. The performances are lively, with more than adequate devils along the lines of medieval painters. You may also see pasties being served for the Last Supper, though certainly at one performance the servant who brought them in was told to take them away as they were for after the performance.

8 Cape Cornwall to Porthcurno

via Sennen Cove and Land's End
11.4 miles (18.4 km)

Cape Cornwall, despite its grand name, is a low, little hummock compared with other mere 'heads' on this coast. The chimney **68** is a navigational mark and was said to have produced too fierce a draught for the tin mine on the south side of the Cape, of which only the counthouse (office) survives. The former coastguard lookout is now manned by Coastwatch.

The Coast Path starts just below the car park, and when on top of the cliff you pass Ballowall Barrow **69**, a large and altered chambered cairn that was once buried under mine waste. The lush Cot Valley sometimes harbours rare birds blown across from America. In living memory the little fields ('quillets') in the valley grew crops of potatoes and other vegetables, and cattle and sheep grazed. Now only a couple of tiny fields are cultivated; the rest is owned by the NT. The youth hostel is the house among the trees on the south side. Formerly the valley was active with mining for tin both underground and from sediment in the valley bottom. The horizontal lines on the valley sides show where there were leats feeding the waterwheels. Near the end of the valley are tin processing works from the Second World War.

The large round boulders in the lower part of the cliff at Porthnanven, where the stream reaches the sea, are very similar in shape and size to the boulders rolled around by storms on the present beach (indeed, some have fallen out of the cliff). Dr Borlase in the 18th century commented on this and now geologists believe that this is an excellent example of a 'fossilised' beach, dating from the last interglacial. It is designated an SSSI. Above the boulders the material is angular and mixed with soil: this is probably frost-shattered material from the succeeding glacial time, when Cornwall would have been tundra.

After leaving the tin-streaming works at the end of Cot Valley, the path is well marked, but take care to follow the zigzag path **A** up the cliff, north of Gribba Point.

On the hill near Polpry Cove you can rest among several tumuli. The soil and the previous occupants have gone and the granite slabs make good seats. To the south lies Whitesand Bay, with the path running along the top of rapidly eroding low cliffs, before you are directed through palisaded dunes. If

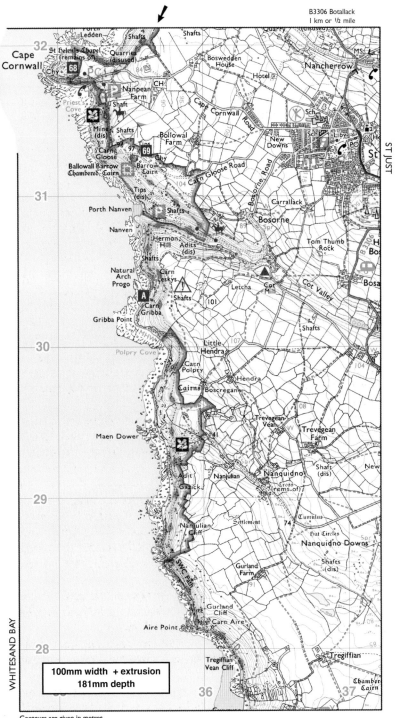

Cape Cornwall

St Helen's Chapel (remains of)

Porth Ledden

Shafts

Shafts

Quarry

Quarries (disused)

68

Chy

Nanpean Farm

Shaft

Cape Cornwall Road

Boswedden House

Hotel

Nancherrow

Sch

New Downs

Bollowal Farm

97

69

Chy

Ballowall Barrow Chambered Cairn

Barrow Cairn

Carn Gloose Road

Liby

PO

St

ST JUST

Carn Gloose

Tips (dis)

Bosorne Road

Carrallack

Porth Nanven

Shafts

Bosorne

Nanven

Hermon Hill

Adits (dis)

Tom Thumb Rock

Cot Valley

Bosa

Shafts

Natural Arch Progo

Carn Leskys

Letcha

Cot Mill

A

Shafts

101

Carn Gribba

Shafts

Gribba Point

Little Hendra

107

Polpry Cove

Carn Polpry

Hendra

Cairns

Boscregan

Maen Dower

41

Trevegean Vean

Trevegean Farm

Shaft (dis)

New

Adit

Gazick

Nanjulian

Nanquidno

Cross (rems.of)

Nanjulian Cliff

Settlement

74

Cumulus

Hut Circles

Nanquidno Downs

Shafts (dis)

SWC Path

Gurland Farm

91

Gurland Cliff

Carn Aire

Aire Point

Tregiffian Vean Cliff

Tregiffian

Chamber Cairn

WHITESAND BAY

36

37

100mm width + extrusion
181mm depth

Contours are given in metres
The vertical interval is 5m

the tide is out and you wish to miss the sea holly and soft sand, it is more pleasant to walk along the beach. It is a popular one for swimming and surfing, but take notice of the lifeguards and any instructions or warnings. The village of Sennen Cove has a pub, The Old Success, cafés, a general store, car parks, a lifeboat station and the circular capstan

A30 Penzance
8 1/2 km or 5 1/4 miles

Contours are given in me
The vertical interval is 5

82

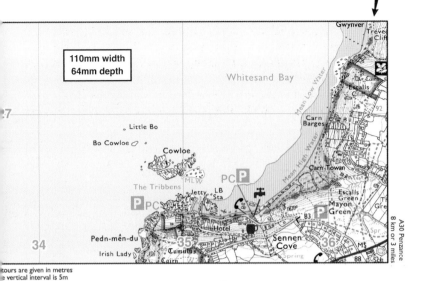

tours are given in metres
e vertical interval is 5m

house, which has been turned into a market. Behind the lifeboat station and the car park a pitched stone path continues up Mayon Cliff, past the old coastguard lookout, which is now a NT information point, and then on an easy, much trampled route to Land's End. Take care if you are walking in misty weather, as many tracks lead to the cliff edge and waymarks are scarce. From Land's End you can look back at the remains of the *Mulheim*, which went aground in Gamper Bay in fine weather in 2003, carrying waste plastic.

At Land's End there is a theme park with several 'attractions' with varying relevance to the location, but the value for the walker may be more in the public conveniences and refreshments, and the possibility of getting some cash (if not, there is a cash machine in the post office in Mayon, a nasty walk along the A30 but reached by a pleasanter footpath from Sennen Cove). In the narrow inlet (a 'zawn' in Cornish) below the wire suspension bridge a range of sea-birds nest, though the theme park's twice weekly fireworks in summer may discourage them. West of Land's End is the Longships Lighthouse, replaced in 1873, and 8 miles (13 km) south-west is the Wolf Rock Lighthouse, which was first lit in 1870. The official Coast Path is waymarked again beyond Greeb Cottage **B**, where there are farm animals but not much land for them to live on.

Once you reach Mill Bay or Nanjizal the crowds have been left behind. At the end of Nanjizal valley are the remains of a water-

83

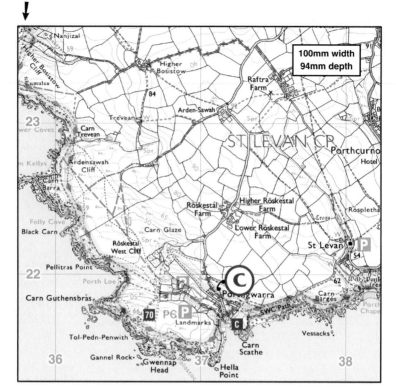

Contours are given in metres
The vertical interval is 5m

mill. After this the path goes to Gwennap Head **70**, possibly named after an obscure Cornish saint, but coastguards knew the lookout as Tol-Pedn or Tol-Pedn-Penwith (the Holed Headland of Penwith). The lookout is now manned by volunteers from Coastwatch (see www.nci.org.uk) and is a 'declared facility'. This means that it is regarded as an integral part of the search and rescue service. Someone is on duty every day of the year from 8am–4pm and longer in summer. There is also an interesting display room downstairs which is open, Easter–October, when the station is staffed, unless, that is, there is an easterly gale, which would probably destroy the contents. Inside you can find out about Coastwatch, about the lighthouses and daymarks, the shipping lanes between Land's End and the Isles of Scilly, and even about local wildlife. The two daymarks help seamen locate the Runnel Stone, scene of many wrecks. If the red cone hides the black-and-white daymark your boat is on the rocks.

Offshore many birds and ships pass to and fro, and in spring and autumn and during south-westerly gales the area is full of birdwatchers, particularly above Hella Point.

84

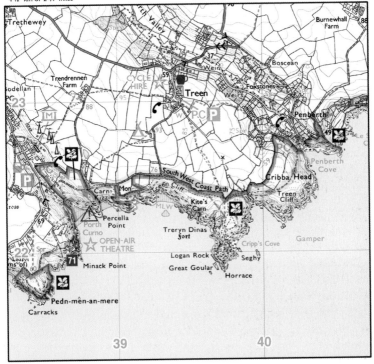

Contours are given in metres
The vertical interval is 5m

The path leaves Porthgwarra by a track in front of the cottages **C**, and not by the seaward track around Carn Scathe. Porth Chapel is a favourite beach, but access is strenuous, so it is less crowded than many. St Levan's Well is beside the path, but the hamlet of St Levan, with its church and a car park in a field, is a few minutes inland.

The Minack Theatre **71** was started in the 1930s. Its setting is similar to the Greek and Roman cliff theatres, but with its pseudo-Celtic designs in cement there is certainly nothing like it in the Mediterranean. A wide range of plays is performed daily in the season by mostly amateur groups; inventive productions staged by the Cornish theatre company, Kneehigh, are in a different class.

Porthcurno is the landfall of a fibre optic cable laid in 1995 and of 14 now disused 'telegraph cables', some dating back to 1870 (see page 86). Much of the award-winning Porthcurno Telegraph Museum is underground in galleries cut in the granite during the Second World War to house the cable terminals. Porth Curno beach is composed of very coarse shell sand, and swimming here is very hazardous because of strong currents.

85

Cornwall and communications

As well as the themes of farming, fishing and mining running as threads through Cornwall's history, the county has had a disparate importance in the history of communications.

In Roman times historians were writing about Belerion and Ictis, which some suggest was St Michael's Mount, and implying that trade was long-standing. Later a multitude of Celtic missionaries from Ireland and Wales came to Cornwall, and some, like Wynwallow, went on to Brittany. These monks, the Cornish saints, set up their chapels by the springs which are now venerated as holy wells. Medieval coastal chapels, usually dedicated to St Nicholas, had the safety of seafarers as one of their concerns and showed a light in a window. In time lighthouses were built and, as trade grew and losses through shipwrecks mounted, further lights filled in the gaps and were built with great difficulty on isolated rocks. Ships which avoided the hazards were guided in by local pilots. Pilot gigs are now enjoying a resurgence as a focus of rivalry between coastal villages like Cadgwith, Porthleven and Padstow, but in the past there were no prizes, and more importantly no pay, for the crew who were runners-up and carried the second pilot to reach the ship.

Falmouth, the most south-westerly safe anchorage in Britain, was the base for the packet boats – fast, armed ships carrying high-value goods for the Post Office – and also the place where ships called in for orders about where to discharge their cargoes for the best prices. Later Lloyd's Signal Station was built on Bass Point and communications between owners and captains became quicker. The Lizard remained the last point for sending messages to outbound ships of the Royal Navy: signallers using semaphore would have been based on hilltops used by signal beacons dating back to long before the Armada.

The growth of submarine telegraphy speeded communications still further. Cables with copper conductors were brought ashore at Porthcurno, Sennen and Kennack. Marconi's experiments with wireless had a major success when his signal ••• ••• ••• ••• from Poldhu was heard at St John's, Newfoundland, in 1901. Intense competition between Marconi's company and the Eastern Telegraph Co. led to an amalgamation as Cable and Wireless, forced by the government which wished both media to prosper. Recent

Pendeen lighthouse filled in the gap between the Longships and Trevose Head.
The keepers' cottages are now holiday lets.

progress in telecommunications in Cornwall has been centred at Goonhilly on Lizard Downs, Britain's first Satellite Earth Station, but in 1995 a new submarine cable, using fibre optics not copper, was brought ashore at Porthcurno, to be followed by others along the Cornish coast.

9 Porthcurno to Penzance

through Mousehole and Newlyn
11.5 miles (18.5 km)

This is a superb coastal walk as far as the coastguard lookout at Penzer Point. From there until Penzance there are different attractions in Mousehole and Newlyn, between which the route runs along a cycle path. Except around Lamorna, the Coast Path mostly keeps to the cliff top, though there are steep drops into each cove.

The path leaves Porth Curno beach up a steep track. Treryn Dinas is famous for the Logan Rock **72**, which is a large block of granite that could be rocked by pushing it gently, until Lieutenant Goldsmith dislodged it in 1824. He was ordered by the Admiralty to replace it, at considerable cost in wages and

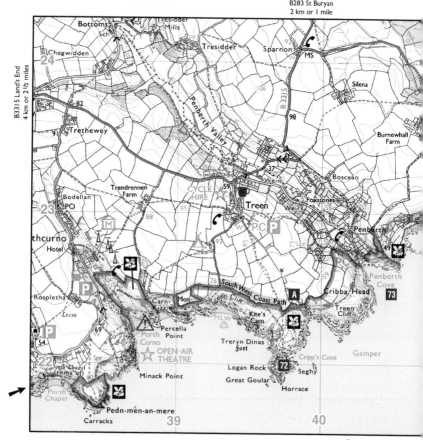

beer, and it now rocks only with difficulty. Many people try to rock other blocks of granite. Just beyond the National Trust collecting box, inside a block of Penryn granite (often used for lighthouses, so plenty strong enough for this job!), the path goes outside the outer rampart **A** of the Iron Age cliff castle, and from here a path leads back to Treen.

Penberth Cove **73** is much photographed and painted, because it is totally unspoilt. There are some boats, a 19th-century capstan, a few cottages, and some very easily missed discreet public conveniences behind the National Trust sign. The path is routed between the seaward cottage and the stream, through the tree mallows. Porthguarnon is even more unspoilt, while St Loy is almost tropical in its lushness. The path here goes along the back of the narrow beach **B** for about 50 yards (45 metres) and, on the very rare occasion, could be difficult with an onshore wind

blowing and a high tide. From the land, Tater-du Lighthouse **74** looks rather insignificant; it first operated in 1965 after this coast had witnessed more than the usual number of wrecks.

Lamorna Cove has several facilities: toilets, café, car park and, further inland, a well-known pub called The Lamorna Wink, originally an illegal beer house.

The old granite quarries here provided stone for the Café Monaco in London's Piccadilly, and for more challenging engineering works such as the Bishop Rock and Wolf Rock lighthouses. The blocks were split by drilling a line of shallow holes, then by putting two wedges in each hole and hammering in a peg between them.

The tiny fields along this stretch of coast were used for early crops, particularly daffodils. Several disused bulb fields are now a coniferous wood **75** – a reserve owned by the Cornwall Wildlife Trust. The path goes through these trees and, shortly after the disused coastguard lookout at Penzer Point, it is routed above the bulb fields for the rest of the way into Mousehole (pronounced 'Mowzul', but named after the cave, The Mousehole).

Point Spaniard **76** is reputed to be where the Spaniards landed in 1595, before destroying Mousehole, Newlyn, Paul

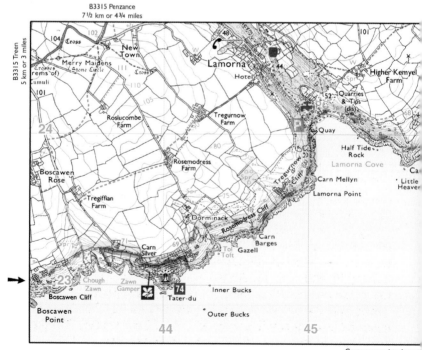

Contours are given in met
The vertical interval is 5r

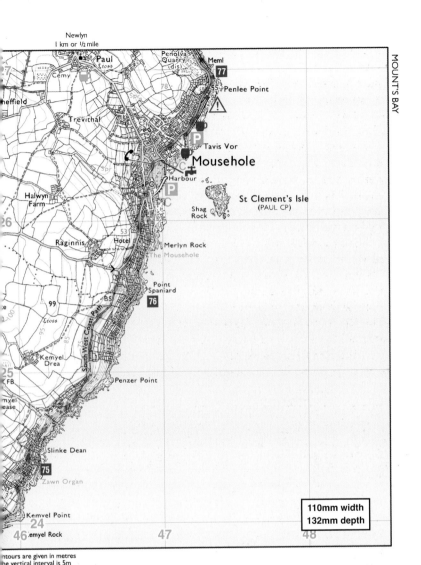

Newlyn
1 km or ½ mile

Contours are given in metres
The vertical interval is 5m

and Penzance. It is traditionally believed that only one building in Mousehole survived their fires – the Keigwin. More recently, a large freezer-trawler, the *Conqueror*, landed on St Clement's Isle on Boxing Day 1977, but she slid off into deep water and can now be seen only by divers. A totally different Christmas tragedy in 1981 was the double loss of the Penlee lifeboat and the coaster *Union Star*, when a rescue attempt failed. Both crews, and the coaster's passengers, were lost. This is commemorated by a small garden at the lifeboat station **77**. The new larger lifeboat is stationed in Newlyn harbour.

Newlyn's harbour has expanded far beyond its small medieval quay.

Newlyn's medieval quay **78** is dwarfed by the newer harbour built for the fishing fleet. Recently many boats have been cut up and scrapped. Yet in 2007, Newlyn still had the second highest-value catch in Britain, apart from the Scottish ports. If you are dismayed by the small range of fish available at your local fish-monger, you should look through the door at a fish auction, usually starting at 8.00am, in the fish market **79** built with finan-cial aid from the EU. Much of the fish goes back to sea – on the Plymouth to Roscoff ferry – to be eaten on the Continent.

Until recently Newlyn had the last pilchard works **80**, the very last vestige of the historic Cornish pilchard fishery (see page 39). Pilchards are still being tinned, and prepared for supermarkets, but on an industrial estate nearby. The Coast Path does not go as far as the main road bridge, but crosses the stream by the Missions to Seamen building, before going down the lane passing seawards of the Newlyn Art Gallery.

Wherry Rocks used to have a tin mine on it, with power being transmitted by flat rods from the engine onshore. The mineshaft had a waterproof structure built up around it, but this was destroyed by a ship drifting in a storm. The mine never reopened. Battery Rocks **81** were just as their name suggests, with suitable guns for coastal defence. The main feature today is the restored Art Deco swimming pool, dating from 1935. Far older are the next buildings: the Barbican, the Dolphin, Coinagehall Street, the old Trinity House building, the Customs House and then the dry dock. More of the district's history is in the excellent museum **82** in Penlee Park.

The railway and bus stations, and the Tourist Information Centre lie close together at the base of Albert Pier.

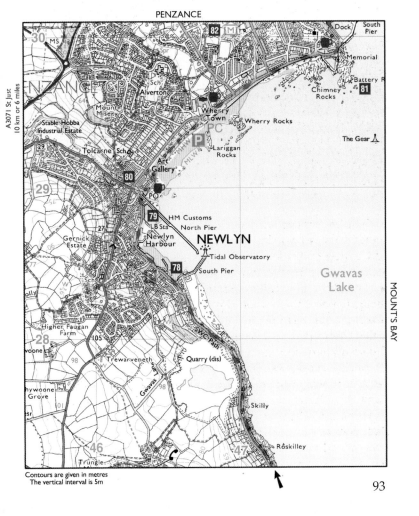

PENZANCE

Contours are given in metres
The vertical interval is 5m

Penzance

Penzance is worth exploring. While cars rush by on one side of the town along the new road towards Land's End, walkers can easily rush by along the sea front, drawn by the obvious attraction of St Michael's Mount, but it is far better to call in at the Tourist Information Centre near the railway station for a free town map and then spend a few hours wandering around the town.

Penzance's visible history is barely 200 years old – no buildings are known to have survived the destruction of the town by the Spaniards in 1595 and most of the buildings around Market Jew Street, the main shopping area, date from the 18th century. The lower side of Market Jew has also seen more recent destruction, but the view up towards the elegant Market House, with the raised pavement known as 'The Terrace' on the right, is still one of the finer pieces of townscape in Cornwall. In front of the Market House stands a statue of Humphry Davy (1778–1829), a local man and the greatest chemist of his day. Davy is most widely known as the inventor of the safety lamp, an invention that saved the lives of innumerable coal miners, who had previously used candles. These frequently ignited the fire-damp, chiefly methane gas, with disastrous results. Methane is generated by coal and is not found in Cornish metal mines.

Behind the Market House you can turn left into Chapel Street to see the extraordinary Egyptian House, built in 1835–36 and now owned by the Landmark Trust. If you retrace your steps to Alverton Street and then follow Morrab Road past the public library, you will reach Penlee Park and the small Penzance and District Museum and Art Gallery. Small it may be, but the gallery has a very good collection of paintings by the Newlyn School of Painters (Stanhope Forbes, Lamorna Birch, Elizabeth Armstrong, Henry Scott Tuke, and others), and upstairs the museum has much to complement what the walker will have seen of the wildlife, antiquities and mining. If you go back up Morrab Road you will come to the imposing old municipal building, St John's Hall, which also houses the Royal Geological Society of Cornwall, the second oldest geological society in Britain, founded in 1814. Sir Humphry Davy was a vigorous supporter, and if the Society had adopted a proposal to sponsor a Professor of Mineralogy, Penzance might well have had a school of mines and even a university – an intriguing thought.

Market Jew Street in Penzance is dominated by the granite Market House. In front is a marble statue of Sir Humphry Davy.

As it was, in 1663 the town had successfully petitioned to become a 'coinage town', testing the purity of all the tin ingots produced in the area, which would then be exported through the port. Formerly the tin had been assayed at Helston and shipped from Gweek. The harbour was also used for the fishing fleet, and Mousehole, Newlyn and Penzance vied for prominence over the centuries. They all suffered from 'Turkish' pirates (in reality slavers from the Barbary Coast of North Africa), who took men, women and children.

In the early 19th century Penzance, with its mild climate, was known as a resort for the gentry, who could not so easily visit the Continent because of hostilities. With the railway connection between Penzance and Paddington in 1866 came tourists and the development of hotels, so that today the port area seems almost divorced from the rest of the town.

Penzance still handles the boats to the Isles of Scilly, as well as having a small dry dock, but most of the fish is landed at Newlyn.

10 Penzance to Porthleven

passing St Michael's Mount and Praa Sands
13.9 miles (22.4 km)

This is an easy stretch and could be undertaken by anyone able to cross stiles and walk along a beach. The path follows part of the National Cycle Network from the end of the bus station **A** nearest the harbour – if you reach the railway station you have gone too far. Marazion Marsh **83** is a well-known site for over-wintering aquatic birds, with a bittern present most winters, as well as a major starling roost most years. In summer rare Cetti's warblers breed. A road runs along the side of the open water in the marsh, so birdwatching is simple, with a helpful board informing you about recent sightings in West Cornwall.

MOUNT'S BAY

St Michael's Mount **84** was a Benedictine Priory before it became a fortress in the 12th century, and later a major port for exporting tin and copper. Much of what you see was remodelled in Victorian times: more Neuschwanstein than military design. The real interest in the Mount is its history before the Benedictines: was it Ictis, a tin-trading port of the first millennium BC mentioned by the Roman Diodorus? Nowadays the National Trust holds it for posterity, and you can reach it by ferry, or on foot across the causeway if the tide is out.

Marazion is sometimes called Market Jew, but originally these were separate places. Market Jew comes from the Cornish '*marghas yow*' or 'Thursday market', and Marazion from '*marghas byghan*' or 'little market'. Both had charters in the 11th century.

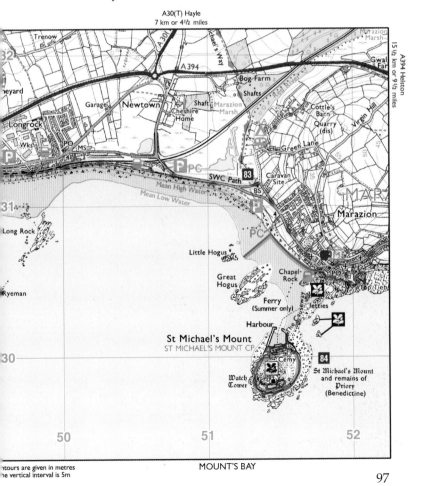

The Coast Path uses the road through Marazion until Henfor Terrace **B**, then returns to the beach for a short stretch. This can be a problem with a high spring tide and a heavy sea; in this case an alternative is to carry on along the road from Marazion, turn right by the cemetery, walk to Perranuthnoe and rejoin the route.

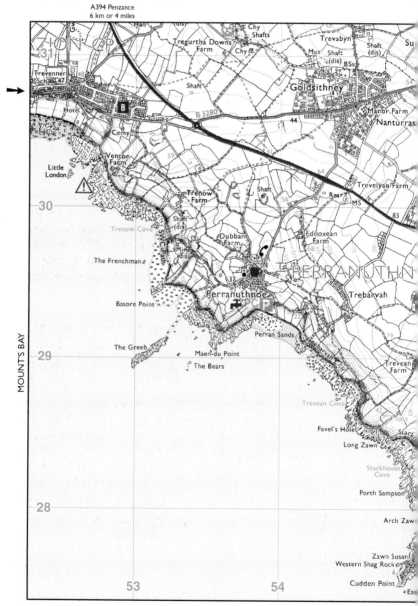

A cliff fall between Trenow Cove and Basore Point has resulted in the Coast Path being diverted inland for a short distance. It wanders along the cliff top and through little fields to Cudden Point. Above the path lies the surprising Acton Castle, built in the grand manner by an industrialist.

In 1947 HMS *Warspite*, *en route* to the breakers, broke free from her tugs near the Wolf Rock and ran aground just offshore. The iron-bound post and chains between Piskies Cove and Bessy's Cove are relics of the salvage, carried out over six years here and at Marazion. She was the largest wreck ever to occur on the Cornish coast; her marine boilers still lie off St Michael's Mount.

Prussia Cove **85** is named after the King of Prussia, alias John Carter, a notorious smuggler. It was originally called Porthleah Cove, but it became the base for the Carter family 'business', with the storage caves in Piskies Cove, and the harbour and the roadway from it in Bessy's Cove: the ruts across the beach bear witness to the scale of the free trade. On the cliff top was a small battery to discourage revenue boats, and nearby was a kiddlywink selling liquor on which duty had not been paid. This was run by Bessy Bussow, in whose honour the cove is named. Porth En Alls **86** is the base for masterclasses of the International Musicians' Seminar, followed by concerts in local churches. Above Kennegy Sand the path crosses the dumps of the Speedwell tin and copper mine **87**; you may find amethyst among the waste.

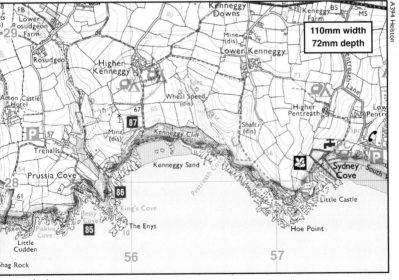

110mm width
72mm depth

Contours are given in met
The vertical interval is 5

If you are leaving Praa Sands, heading towards Penzance, you will find the path seaward of the bungalows **C** to the west of the pub on the beach. If going the other way, the path is on the beach **D** in front of the pub, but the official route is then up the next steps and along the seaward side of the car park.

Above Porthcew stands the Wheal Prosper engine house **88**, owned by the National Trust, while below on the beach and in the cliffs the contact line between the granite and the slate can be seen. The two engine houses near Trewavas Head are also now owned by the NT, but most of the mining took place much further inland near, or on, Tregonning Hill.

Porth Sulinces lies not on granite but on slate, and this gives rise to a continual problem with landslips. For your own safety keep to the waymarked or fenced path and take notice of any cracks opening up in the ground.

Just east of Tregear Point is a monument **89** to all drowned men, women and children who, prior to the Grylls Act of 1808, were buried on the cliffs, rather than in consecrated ground. On the beach below is the Giant Rock, made of garnet-gneiss, and quite different from all the other rocks in Cornwall, but similar to rocks in Greenland. How – and when – it got here is a matter of debate. Most geologists think it was dropped by a melting iceberg, but differences in sea level need explaining. It, and the area around it, is now protected as a Site of Special Scientific Interest.

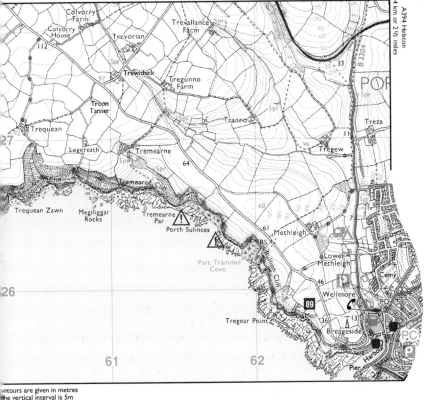

ntours are given in metres
the vertical interval is 5m

Porthleven is a fishing village with a pleasant dockside. Many of its old buildings, some dating from the early 18th century, are still intact and put to modern uses. Most of the new building, mainly to house families connected with the Culdrose helicopter base, has been kept away from the old part of the village.

11 Porthleven to Lizard

through Polurrian Cove
14.1 miles (22.6 km)

This section is generally easy walking on the top of the cliffs, with a few steep-sided coves to cross. The main hazard is likely to be stiles made of serpentine, which walkers' boots polish and which become treacherous when they are wet.

The path leaves Porthleven by the castellated town council building with its clock-tower, and uses the lane through the village until the car park at the entrance to the Penrose Estate, owned by the National Trust. (If you are coming from the Lizard and heading for Porthleven, leave the beach by the rough road at the start of the cliffs **A** and do not take short cuts: the old, direct route has fallen away.) If you wish to visit Helston (see page 110) there are paths on both sides of the Loe, but the western path is reached from the drive.

The Loe **90** (*loe* is a Cornish word for pool) is the largest natural body of fresh water in Cornwall and had formed by 1301, when a document records that Helston was no longer a port because of the growth of the sand bar.

Swimming on either side of the bar is not recommended. The Loe receives water rich in phosphate and nitrate and so suffers from periodic blooms of toxin-producing blue-green algae, while the sea usually has a strong undertow. It is far better to keep your feet dry and to enjoy the sea holly, the rare yellow horned poppy and other plants rooted among the inhospitable gravel. Legend has it that the bar was formed when the giant Tregeagle dropped some sand from a sack that he was carrying. Tregeagle was a 17th-century inhuman land steward of the Robartes family from Lanhydrock near Bodmin. He was said to have been summoned from the dead to be a witness in a court case, but could not be returned to the dead and so was given impossible tasks, such as removing all the sand from a particularly sandy cove. Another legend with chronological problems has Excalibur, King Arthur's sword, being thrown into the Loe.

Above the bar is a memorial **91** to the 100 or so people who were drowned, and buried in the fields, after HMS *Anson* was beached in a storm in 1807. The local people were powerless to help and a young cabinetmaker called Henry Trengrouse resolved to design a system that might have saved their lives. In 1808 he invented a rocket with a line attached that could be fired from either a ship or the shore. At great personal cost his

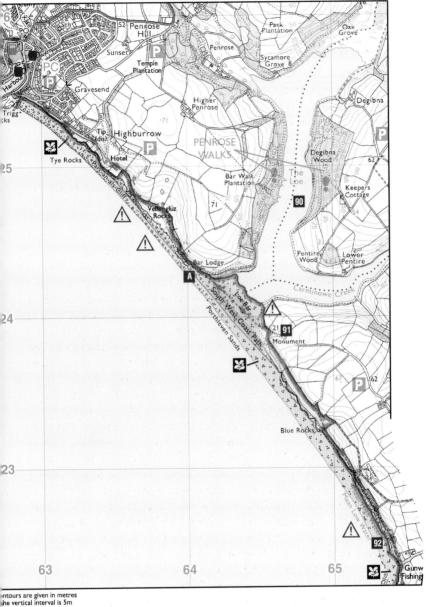

Contours are given in metres
The vertical interval is 5m

breeches buoy system was adopted, and he died penniless in
1854. The grateful government had awarded him £20.

Further along, one of the windlasses **92** possibly came from
the 1890 wreck of the *Brankelow*. When storms scour the sand

off the rocks you can see innumerable bits of wrecks along this coast. Sailing ships used to run for safety from sou'westerly gales into Mount's Bay, but when the wind veered sou'easterly they were trapped.

The cliff is slipping here so you need to heed any re-routing of the path and follow the waymarks, while above Halzephron ('cliff of hell') Cove even the road has slipped and been re-routed.

Winnianton **93** was a Saxon royal manor and figures large in Domesday, but today visitors come seeking the tranquillity of Gunwalloe Church, and maybe to look for gold coins from the Spanish and Dutch wrecks on this storm-battered coast.

To the south of the large hotel, now a retirement home, above Poldhu Cove is the remains of Marconi's wireless station **94**, from where the first transatlantic radio message was sent in 1901 (see page 86). In 2001 the National Trust opened the Marconi Centre at the end of the field. This is the home of Poldhu Amateur Radio Club and is open to the public regularly throughout the year. The next cove south is Polurrian Cove, and from either the cove or the large hotel above it a short walk leads into Mullion with its church with 16th-century carved bench-ends. Mullion Cove is 2 miles (3.2 km) from the centre of Mullion.

The yellow-horned poppy, with its long sickle-shaped seed pods, grows among the flinty gravel of Loe Bar.

The granite and serpentine harbour at Mullion Cove is only of Victorian age. It is now owned by the National Trust.

Mullion Island, made of lava that erupted on the sea bed around 350 million years ago, is the most important nesting site for birds on the Lizard; cormorants, shags, kittiwakes and black-backed gulls are the main tenants. South of Mullion is a National Nature Reserve **95** (see page 111) managed by Natural England, and inland the Cornwall Wildlife Trust has two reserves totalling 272 acres (110 hectares) on the downs north and south of Predannack Airfield. The reserves have a European designation as a Natura 2000 site. The airfield is used mostly for helicopter training, and the partially dismembered corpses of aircraft visible from the Coast Path are kept for firefighting and for practising removal of people from crashed planes.

Gew-graze **96** makes a sheltered spot to stop, as the path drops from the flat downs into the valley. Soapstone was quarried here and sent to the potteries before the Cornish china clay

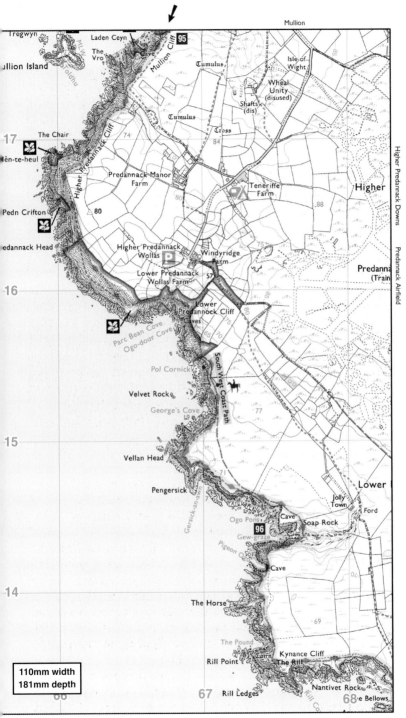

Mullion

Tregwyn
Laden Ceyn
95
The Vro
Cave
Mullion Island
Tumulus
Isle of Wight
Wheal Unity (disused)
Shafts (dis)
Cross
The Chair
17
74
84
Ên-te-heul
Higher Predannack Cliff
Predannack Manor Farm
Teneriffe Farm
Higher
88
Pedn Crifton
80
80
Predannack Head
Higher Predannack Wollas
Windyridge Farm
Predanna (Train
Lower Predannack Wollas Farm
57
16
Lower Predannock Cliff
Caves
Parc Bean Cove
Ogo-dour Cove
65
70
Pol Cornick
South West Coast Path
Velvet Rock
77
George's Cove
L9
15
Vellan Head
71
Pengersick
Jolly Town
Lower
Ford
Gensick-an-vavn
Ogo Pons
Cave
Soap Rock
96
Gew-graze
Pigeon O
The Horse
69
14
The Pound
Cairn
Kynance Cliff
Rill Point
The Rill
110mm width
181mm depth
66
67
Rill Ledges
68 e Bellows
Nantivet Rock

Higher Predannack Downs
Predannack Airfield

ntours are given in metres
he vertical interval is 5m

107

industry began. Back on the downs, the twin towers of the Lizard lighthouse come into view before the path drops into Kynance Cove **97**. The cove has been a much-loved tourist spot since Victorian times. Prince Albert, Queen Victoria's consort, brought their children here in 1846. Since he had a reputation for promoting science and technology he would no doubt be pleased by the 'green' technology installed by the National Trust in 2004: solar tiles on roofs, and a self-contained sewage system for café waste and the new public conveniences. Previously the NT had tackled the erosion problems caused by the 150,000 visitors each year by building paths of local stone. The islands and beaches are accessible at low water, but there is a great risk of being cut off as the tide rises. Wild asparagus is found on Asparagus Island, and the two sheltered valleys leading to the cove contain a wealth of the special flora of the Lizard, such as bloody cranesbill and thyme broomrape. The origin of the name 'Kynance' is much debated. Some suggest that it comes from *ky* – dog in Cornish, and suggest wild dogs roamed in the valleys (*nans*). But it is more likely that Kynance comes from *kynans,* meaning a ravine, as there's a similar word – *ceunant* – in Welsh. Certainly the fanciful English names for the rocks and the caves are Victorian inventions. The old settlement **98**, just above the western valley, dates from the Bronze and Iron Ages so provides no help in the origin of the name.

Lizard Point, called Lizard Head on all old maps (and now called Old Lizard Head by the NT!), is the western side of the headland, and a good area to spot choughs (see page 112). To the east, where the road from Lizard town (see page 110) ends, are cafés and a plaque with the service record of the Lizard lifeboats, while down in exposed Polpeor Cove is the former lifeboat station **99**. Lizard Point Youth Hostel is in the former Polbrean Hotel. The lighthouse was built in 1751 and you will need to look at www.trinityhouse.co.uk to see visiting times for the current year. Both towers used to exhibit a light, so distinguishing the Lizard from Scilly's one light and the three lights of Le Casquet in Jersey. Before chronometers were available ships could find their latitude fairly accurately by measuring the height of the sun but longitude was problematical, so the different lights helped vessels entering the Channel. Nowadays sailors recognise lights by the pattern, duration and colour of their flashes, but most navigation is done using GPS, with the older radio-based LORAN as a rapidly declining back-up.

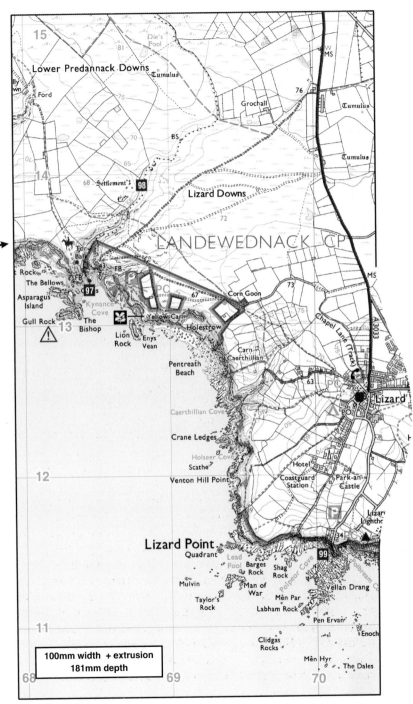

100mm width + extrusion
181mm depth

Contours are given in metres
The vertical interval is 5m

JUST OFF THE PATH: *Helston*

Helston was formerly a stannary town, where tin ingots had to be taken to be assayed. A corner ('coign') of each ingot was removed and tested for purity, and both Helston and Penzance have Coignage Hall Streets.

Helston is known today for the annual Furry Dance on 8 May, when the townsfolk dance in their finest through the streets and in and out of houses. The 'Floral Dance' tune has been arranged by several musicians, and recorded by numerous bands and orchestras, and many people in Britain would start humming along if you played a recording.

The town is also known as the birthplace of Henry Trengrouse, who invented the rocket-powered lifesaving apparatus which later became the breeches buoy (see page 102), and also of Bob Fitzsimmons, a local blacksmith who went on to become a most unlikely world boxing champion whose career spanned both the bare-knuckle era and the later use of gloves. Most unlikely because he weighed less than 12 stone, was knock-kneed and spindly-legged, but knocked down fighters weighing 4 stones more: 'The bigger they come, the harder they fall,' he is reputed to have said.

In the main street The Blue Anchor pub is honoured by beer-drinkers, real beer-drinkers, because when the big breweries stopped making real ale, preferring to produce fizzy, dead keg beers which were easy to store (but had few other virtues), The Blue Anchor continued to brew various strengths of Spingo. Pilgrims still visit this hallowed spot, as Spingo is still brewed by successive landlords.

Just off the other end of the main street is the excellent town museum, which is probably best visited before The Blue Anchor. Here in the old butter and meat markets, and extended into the drill hall, are very well-presented displays of Helston's history.

JUST OFF THE PATH: *Lizard Town*

'Lizard Town' seems rather grand for a sprawling village which is the centre of the cottage industry in turning serpentine. After inspecting the various shops, a logical next step is to visit the pub, The Top House, which has a display of the many varieties of serpentine which have been used at different times. It also is one of probably only two pubs with serpentine beer-pump handles, and has a spectacular collection of photographs connected with the Lizard lifeboats. There are only a handful of serpentine turners left, and the supply of serpentine of adequate quality is nearly exhausted. Every time any of the utility companies digs a trench in a possible area, the serpentine turners go in hope to look. The largest pieces made are usually models of lighthouses. While large enough blocks of serpentine are found for use in houses and even in church walls, the cracks in serpentine bodies are too close together to allow the massive dove-tailed blocks of rock used in making lighthouses. A short walk from the centre of the village towards Church Cove takes you to Landewednack church. This has a chequered tower of granite and serpentine, and also a Victorian lectern of serpentine. If you take other walks from the village you may find you are directed on to a right-of-way on top of a double-width hedge, somewhat of a Lizard speciality, though these are also found in Brittany.

The Lizard

The Lizard is unique. This uniqueness arises mainly from the geology, but also from the mild oceanic climate and the flatness of the land. Geologists think the Lizard is an 'ophiolite' – a piece of ocean floor which has been thrust up. The Lizard is famous for its serpentine, which is thought to be a slightly altered slab of the Earth's mantle, the zone between the crust and the molten core. On the poorly drained plateau that makes up most of the Lizard, this rock produces poor, thin soils rich in magnesium. On these grow Cornish heath, western gorse, bell heather and some rarities, with a distinctive set of plants including more rarities on the salt-sprayed clifftop heathland. The jumbled mass of colourfully streaked rock on the coast gives rise to such long-standing tourist attractions as Kynance Cove.

The rock is also the source material for the Lizard's cottage industry of making turned stone ornaments, but in the industry's fashionable Victorian heyday what can only be described as a factory developed at Poltesco, with an export business and a London office.

The other rocks on the Lizard include schist and gneiss, formed under very high pressures and temperatures within the Earth. These give rise to better soils with a quite different natural flora, as well as very abrupt changes in land use where they are in contact with the serpentine. Naturalists know the Lizard not only for its flowers, but also for some rare insects and the major breeding colonies of seabirds on the cliffs.

Natural England has designated many parts of the Lizard as SSSIs, and large areas are included in the Lizard National Nature Reserve. The National Trust owns much of the coast and has covenants on further stretches, and the Cornwall Wildlife Trust has two large nature reserves. Since it is truly a unique area, one can only hope that with these safeguards it is protected from any further damage by insensitive tourism, farming and neglect.

Choughs

The chough is an emblematic bird for the Cornish; indeed some would go so far as saying it is their national bird, just as the black-and-white cross of St Piran is the Cornish flag, seen flying outside County Hall and many other places, and on thousands of stickers on the backs of cars. A chough stands on top of the coat of arms of the county of Cornwall, while the arms are supported by a fisherman and a miner. But in 1973 the last resident chough died. Choughs had suffered a long decline, having been abundant all along the south coast from Dover to Cornwall in the 17th century, but by 1802 they were chiefly confined to Devon, Cornwall and Wales. And as they became rarer so their eggs were more desirable in collections, and stuffed choughs began to grace the houses of the gentry, such as Lanhydrock, whereas before some had had them as pets.

At the end of the 20th century research was begun into what choughs needed, with the idea that these conditions could be recreated and choughs re-introduced. Choughs in the UK live on the coast and probe into short grass for food, but much of the coastal slope had scrubbed over, so a lot of effort was put into clearing some scrub and using cattle and Shetland ponies to check regrowth; grazing also helps to bring back coastal wild flowers. In addition to short or open grass, choughs feed on insects found in cowpats and stubble fields, so a mosaic of habitat was recreated by farmers, supported by Stewardship schemes. Then in 2001 three wild choughs arrived on the Lizard and stayed, effectively re-introducing themselves. A pair bred in 2002, and by 2008 they and subsequent pairs have successfully reared 38 chicks (there is a high mortality rate for young choughs, but in Cornwall their survival rate is very good). Members of the

With their all black plumage, red bills and red legs, choughs are distinctly different to the more common jackdaws.

original group are also flying to Land's End and Porthgwarra, so there is hope that the choughs really are back. Vigilance is still, sadly, needed as known egg collectors have had to be warned away by the police. Details about the Cornwall Chough Project (a partnership between RSPB, National Trust and Natural England) can be found on the RSPB website (www.rspb.org.uk).

Choughs can now be seen around the Lizard and Land's End peninsulas, and north to Pendeen. In Spring at Most Southerly Point on the Lizard there is a chough watchpoint manned by an RSPB warden most days in April to mid-June, where you can experience the choughs' distinctive call, and see their aerobatic flight as this is where the original pioneering pair have continued nesting. Certainly if you ask many people on the Lizard they will be able to tell you exactly where the choughs have been seen recently, and their complete family history. Sadly the miner on Cornwall's coat of arms is impossible to re-introduce, except as a tourist spectacle, and the fisherman seems to be following the miner.

Squeezed into its narrow cove and valley, Cadgwith is protected from all but south-east

...es.

12 Lizard to Coverack

via Cadgwith
10.4 miles (16.7 km)

The route is easy as far as Cadgwith, but from there to Coverack there are a few tiring climbs and steep slippery slabs of rock to cross. This really is the geological walk par excellence.

The route starts from the cafés and serpentine shop above the old lifeboat station **99** in Polpeor Cove. The rock collector can easily obtain most varieties of serpentine from the shop's waste, although the serious geologist will want to see the varieties *in situ* and will need a proper geological guide to the area. In Polpeor Cove by the old lifeboat house you will find gneiss, but the Coast Path is on schist, as you pass south of the most southerly house, past Housel Bay, to Church Cove.

The slopes of Bass Point are covered with Hottentot fig – an unwelcome alien, because the mass of stems chokes the native flora. The inside of the ripe fruit is edible – but please do not spread the seed or pieces of stem. Between Housel Bay and Bass Point are the restored Lizard Wireless Station **100** and Lloyd's Signal Station **101**, from where incoming ships were given visual orders about their movements (see page 86). Coastwatch mans the old coastguard lookout, and will record your passing.

In 1961 the lifeboat was moved from Polpeor Cove to the more sheltered station in Kilcobben Cove **102**, which can be visited Monday–Friday in the mornings. Church Cove has not only an old capstan house but also a fish palace. A worthwhile diversion here is to walk up the valley as far as St Wynwallow's Church **103** at Landewednack (Church Cove village on the map). This has a Norman door, though most of the church dates from the 14th–15th centuries. The tower is chequered with serpentine and granite. St Guénolé (St Samson) was abbot of Landevennac in Brittany, and Gunwalloe Church is also dedicated to him.

The serpentine quarries to the north of Church Cove provided stone for the runways at Culdrose airfield, and crushed serpentine has also been used for firebricks.

Further on, the rock underfoot is schist, a black sparkling rock with fine white layers, which has been quarried above Chough's Ogo **104**, leaving a very comfortable resting place on the rock; sadly there have been no choughs to watch here for 150 years, but now that choughs are breeding nearby that may change. Further on a wooden seat has been provided, so that you can sit and look down into Hugga Driggee, more commonly known

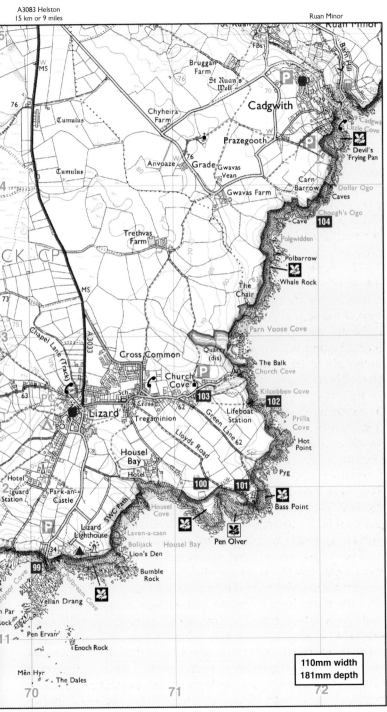

110mm width
181mm depth

...tours are given in metres
...e vertical interval is 5m

Contours are given in me
The vertical interval is

nowadays by its very fanciful English name of the Devil's Frying Pan, a funnel-shaped depression with a natural arch at the bottom. At one stage in their naming and renaming of natural features the Victorians were calling Hugga Driggee (*Hugga/Ogo* – a cave in Cornish) the Devil's Frying Pan, the Devil's Punch Bowl and the Devil's Cauldron! The Coast Path winds through a private garden, then turns right to pass on the seaward side of the cottages. Cadgwith is many people's idea of a proper Cornish fishing village. It lost its lifeboat when the new lifeboat station was built at Kilcobben, taking the place of both the Cadgwith and the Lizard boats, and the old pilchard cellars are now a café. On the north side of Cadgwith Cove the small hut with the chimney was a coastguard lookout.

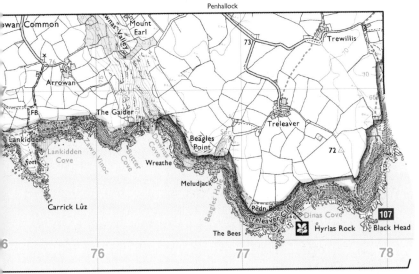

ours are given in metres
vertical interval is 5m

Poltesco **105** is the site of an old serpentine works, from where the pulpit in Landewednack Church came. The water-powered serpentine factory took over the site from a pilchard seine (see page 39), which had built the rounded building as a capstan house for hauling in boats and nets. The pilchard operation went back to Elizabethan times. The fortunes of the serpentine works improved enormously in 1846 when Queen Victoria ordered a serpentine fireplace for Osborne House on the Isle of Wight.

Kennack Sands **106** is a popular beach, with many caravan sites nearby, as well as beach cafés, a car park and public conveniences. Geologically the south end is interesting because of its complexity: the enigmatic Kennack gneiss, serpentine and gabbro, all within a few yards of each other. There are veins of asbestos here, and also veins of talc, though not enough for a local cottage industry to produce Lizard talcum powder. On the east side of Kennack Sands, after the concrete bridge, the path follows a lane seaward of the trees. It goes through an area of butcher's broom, growing on the alkaline soil, and you should find some Cornish Heath. Then on to Lankidden, with its tiny sandy beach and a track to the road, which could be useful for anyone who wished to miss the steep climb and descent at Downas Cove.

On a clear day it is obvious why a coastguard lookout was placed at Black Head **107**, as walkers from the Lizard can see Falmouth, the Dodman, and more headlands beyond.

119

At Chynhalls Cliff there is a length of path on a boardwalk through a reed bed, with a spur **A** running out to the Iron Age 'fort' at Chynhalls Point.

The main Coast Path goes down seaward of the Wesleyan Chapel, and then hugs the coast round Dolor Point and the Paris Hotel, going past the old lifeboat station to the small harbour. Coverack boasts a youth hostel, cafés, shops, post office, excellent ice-cream (at the sign of the dancing cow!), a bus service to Helston, and an exposure of the Moho (the Earth's mantle/crust boundary) on the beach.

The Duchy of Cornwall

Some people refer to Cornwall as a duchy, but this is a fallacy. The estate known as the Duchy of Cornwall was created in 1337 to provide an income for the heir to the throne. Only a small amount of Cornwall is included, although there are substantial mineral rights which are worth almost nothing today

Poltesco was the base for a pilchard seine before the serpentine factory was developed there in Victorian times.

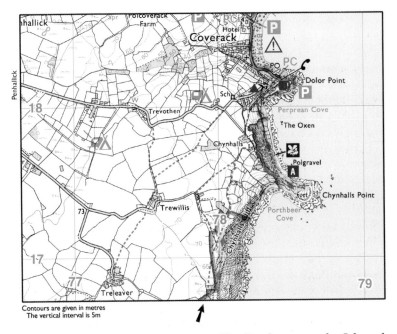

Contours are given in metres
The vertical interval is 5m

as there is no longer any mining. The Duchy owns the Isles of Scilly, but outside Cornwall there are many properties, including Dartmoor Prison and The Oval cricket ground in London.

So the Duchy of Cornwall is completely different to the County of Cornwall, which has about half a million inhabitants – though there are millions more across the world with Cornish roots, whose ancestors left when mining had one of its periodic downturns. Many Cornish see Cornwall as a Celtic nation, alongside Scotland, Wales, Ireland, Man and Brittany, each with a Celtic language. There are certainly some legal oddities which set Cornwall apart from the rest of the United Kingdom, though it has not had its own kings for one thousand years.

Irrespective of its history and status, Cornwall today is one of the most economically deprived areas within the European Union, and because of the low wages gained Objective One status which meant it had funds from Europe which were matched by UK government money to develop the economy. The irony of Cornwall is that it has what is considered to be one of the best environments for work and leisure in the UK, so businesses move their operations to Cornwall (which provides much needed jobs), but also people from wealthier areas buy second homes for their leisure, putting the price of property out of the reach of local people on low wages.

13 Coverack to Falmouth

via Porthallow and Helford
22.9 miles (36.7 km)

This is a longer stretch than the previous chapters, and you may wish to split it in two, especially if the tide is wrong and you have to walk around Gillan Creek. However, the section from the Helford River to Falmouth is an easy one.

From Coverack's small harbour the path follows the road around the back of the beach, then goes along the lane between the houses, until a footpath leaves this lane just before the sewage-treatment works. Follow this footpath and descend towards the beach. The flat expanse of ground behind Lowland Point, finally backed by a steep slope, is a good place to convince doubters that our present sea level is only transitory. During an interglacial, a warm spell during the Ice Age, the sea is thought to have been higher than at present, because less of the Earth's water would have been in the form of ice. The low, flat ground is a raised beach, now covered with soil and abundant chamomile, and the steep slope is the old cliff. The path now traverses Dean Quarries (Gabbro) **108**, and for your own safety you *must* follow the waymarked route, as it is liable to

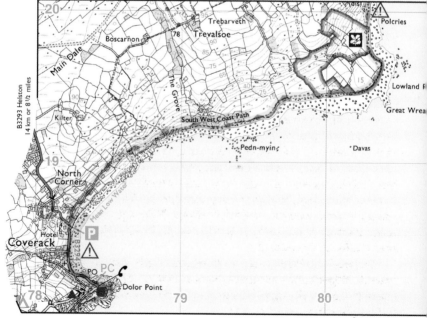

Contours are given in met
The vertical interval is 5r

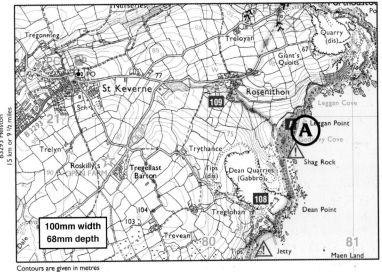

Contours are given in metres
The vertical interval is 5m

change when the rock is quarried. Red flags are flown on both the north and the south ends of the site (marked by warning triangles on the map above) and a hooter sounds continuously if blasting is imminent: you must observe these warnings. In recent years quarrying activity has been much reduced.

The offshore rocks due east of the quarry are the notorious Manacles, the scene of many shipwrecks. Probably the best known is the *Mohegan*, which struck at night in a squally southerly wind in 1898 just as the passengers were sitting down to dinner. Over 100 of her passengers and crew are buried in St Keverne churchyard.

The Coast Path turns inland **A** at the north end of Godrevy Cove and up the track to Rosenithon. Barns in the farmyard **109** are made of rock and cob (mud) with shillet (small pieces of slate). Normally cob walls are plastered and painted over to keep out the wet, so that the composition of the wall is not visible. Cob cottages, the local mud huts, are very comfortable to live in, with superb insulation properties and a large 'thermal mass', so that once the walls are warmed through in winter the temperature of the cottage changes only slowly, while in summer the inside stays cool.

On reaching Porthoustock, the Coast Path once again turns inland. Negotiations are under way and it is hoped that a more coastal route will soon become available. Meanwhile, please follow the waymarked route.

On both sides of Porthoustock, care has been taken to make the path follow fields wherever possible, so on the south side the path crosses a hedge **B** into a field just above the former coastguard houses, while on the north the path follows a level track **C** just in front of some cottages. Where the path leaves the road again it follows the side of Porthallow Vineyard, where you can see apple mills and cider presses.

Porthallow (locally known as Pr'alla) village has a bus service, stores, a café and a pub called The Five Pilchards with lots of ship models as well as serpentine beer pump handles. The village has a large car park, otherwise called the beach and available at all states of the tide. Just east of the pebbly beach a scramble across the varied rocks provides a wealth of interest for anyone interested in geology. Those whose interest is purely aesthetic will enjoy the contortions of the layers in the wet schist boulders, and the colours of the serpentine.

North of Porthallow, past the intriguingly named Snail's Creep (there is a Cornish dance of the same name), you come to a small headland **110** with access to rich rock pools. From here you can see the narrow raised beach that stretches all the way back to Porthallow. The rocks here form the boundary between the exotic rocks of the Lizard – the schists, gneiss and serpentine found nowhere else in Cornwall – and the slates, which with the granite make up most of the rest of the county. The boundary is a zone of squeezed-out material – from pebbles to vast boulders – set in slate. Some of the boulders can be seen 50 yards (45 metres) south of the grassy point. Was this part of a gigantic mud and rock slide over 350 million years ago?

Nare Head claimed one of the largest four-masted clippers then afloat, the *Bay of Panama*, in a blizzard in March 1891. The ship was carrying jute from Calcutta to Dundee and would have dwarfed the *Cutty Sark*, the tea clipper that is preserved at Greenwich. The wreck was found by a farmer who was looking for his sheep in snowdrifts. He summoned the Coverack Rocket Brigade, who rescued 18 of the crew by breeches buoy.

At Gillan Creek, the water is only ankle deep at low tide, but the official route goes around the head of the creek. The boat-hire firm runs a water-taxi and is used to being hailed by walkers. Alternatively you will need to backtrack and follow the directions on the nearby information board **D**, walking up through Flushing towards Manaccan, from where you might

110mm width + extrusion
181mm depth

Dennis Head

Little Dennis

BOAT TRIPS

The Crook

Mên-aver Point

Gillan

Hotel

Spr

Spr

Spr

Lestowder

Trewarnevas

99

76

FB

Roskorwell

Treglossick

Halwyn

FB

49 P

Tregarne

Pengarrock

23

91

Tregarne Mill

16

60

Tredinnick

30

79

Treleague

22

76

Tregonning

06

Mên-aver Beach

Parbean Cove

Lestowder Cliff

40

55

33

Pennare House

Pennare Barton

FB

75

South West Coast Path

Porthallow

46

Tregaminion

69

Trenoweth Mill

Trenoweth Farm Nurseries

80

Treloyan

Nare Point

Observation Post (MOD)

Polnare Cove

Nare Head

110

Nare Cove

Snail's Creep

Fletching's Cove

Nelly's Cove

Gallentreath

Porthallow Cove

PC

Pol Lawrance

Pol Gwarra

Pedn Tiere

Porthkerris Point
Quay

Drawna Roc

Observation Post
(MOD)

Porthkerris

Porthkerris
Cove

PC P

Radar Station
(MOD)

Penc.

St Keverne Quarries
(disused)

Trenance

Chyreen

Batty's Point

C

B

P

Porthoustock

Port

Quarry
(dis)

81

70

contours are given in metres
he vertical interval is 5m

125

wish to go directly to Helford rather than walk along the road on the north side of the creek. St Anthony-in-Meneage occupies what was probably one of the earliest Christian sites in Cornwall. Meneage (pronounced Menayg or Meneeg), 'land of monks', is mentioned in the 10th century.

Just above the church the Coast Path goes through a gate **E** to enter the Bosahan Estate, and it is worth going on to Dennis Head, where there is not only a prehistoric earthwork but also a square Royalist fortification **111** with gun emplacements at the corners. The whole site is rather overgrown.

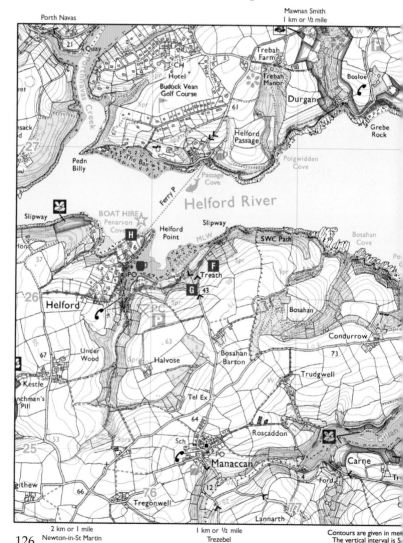

Newton-in-St Martin

Just beyond the junction **F** at Treath the path follows the tarmac road and appears to be heading for the shore, so it is easy to miss the narrow track heading off behind Treath Cottage **G**. You should follow this track, which passes Helford's main car park, before entering the part of the village where all cars (apart from the residents' own) are banned. A stroll along the road past the post office and purveyors of cream teas brings you to the pub, The Shipwright's Arms, and then along a drive to the ferry **H**. A group can summon the ferryman by swinging open the semicircular black board to make a brightly coloured circle.

Mawnan Smith
I km or ½ mile

Contours are given in metres
The vertical interval is 5m

Many people watch the boats from the ferry point, so the ferry-man will only come across if he sees the circle, unless of course he has southbound passengers. The normal service is hourly. For details see page 138.

The inlets off the Helford River include Frenchman's Creek, which gave its name to Daphne du Maurier's novel, and Porthnavas Creek, home of the oyster beds and also mussels and clams. Nearby Gweek was a major port in medieval and later times, from which tin was exported. In the past the river was also infamous for an infestation of pirates.

Once you have crossed the Helford River, the final stage is a gentle walk to Falmouth. The Coast Path follows the road in front of Helford Passage, then goes along the back of the beach into the fields, and passes the gardens of Trebah Manor, famous for Asian and Australian plants. It then enters Durgan village, at the foot of Glendurgan, a sheltered garden full of camellias and azaleas, and also a laurel maze, owned by the National Trust. The path is easy walking through fields past Mawnan, with much bare soil beneath the holm oaks, Rosemullion Head and Gatamala Cove, named after a wreck, to Maenporth

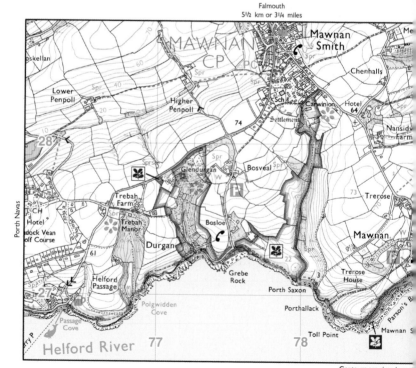

Contours are given in me
The vertical interval is 5

('stony landing-place'). At Mawnan the church tower is used as a landmark to keep sailors clear of the dreaded Manacles: there was even a proposal to paint it white.

There are cafés and public conveniences at Maenporth. The path on either side of the cove goes through an exuberance of old man's beard – wild clematis. In a tiny cove **112** lies the wreck of the *Ben Asdale*, an Aberdeen trawler that went ashore in a gale in December 1978. Her main winch came from the *Conqueror*, wrecked near Mousehole in 1977. In the 1970s large shoals of mackerel were coming close inshore in winter, attracting trawlers

from all over Europe, with much of the catch being sold for fish-meal, direct to Eastern European and Russian factory ships anchored in Falmouth Bay. Eventually a quota system was introduced which meant that when boats netted a big shoal they would first dump an earlier catch that was under quota. Today both pilchards and mackerel are gone, but the much disliked quota system, whereby boats are allowed to catch up to specified amounts of one or more fish, is still in place. So fish are still dumped if a boat has caught in excess of its quota – or caught a type of fish for which it has no quota.

At Pennance Point **113**, with its monument to Falmouth's Home Guard, is the end of the flue from the old arsenic refinery **114**, built on the site of a lead smelter.

Contours are given in me
The vertical interval is 5

The Coast Path joins the tarmac highway about 90 yards (80 metres) from the café above the south end of Swanpool Beach. Swanpool (probably 'swamp-pool' rather than the more graceful connotation) was the site of a lead-silver mine that was active in the 18th century and finally closed in 1860.

The Coast Path continues along Cliff Road and Castle Drive around Pendennis Point. If you wish to visit Pendennis Castle **115**, the entrance is up the hill from the road junction **I**.

The name Pendennis, 'headland of a fort', implies an Iron Age promontory-fort, but only more modern defences are now visible here. South of Crab Quay is a small Tudor blockhouse, Little Dennis, which originally had four guns at ground level. Pendennis Castle was built in 1540–43 as one of a chain stretching from Hull to Milford Haven, for defence against an expected combined fleet from the Pope, King Charles I of Spain (also Holy Roman Emperor) and the King of France. This unlikely alliance of erstwhile enemies was brought about by Henry VIII's Dissolution of the Monasteries, his declaration of himself as head of the Church, and his attempts to rid himself of his first wife, Catherine of Aragon (Charles's aunt). That accounted for the Pope and the Emperor: the French joined in because they were the traditional enemy of England anyway!

The massive star-shaped defences around the castle were built by Elizabeth I, and the whole complex's finest hour came with its five-month defence against fellow-countrymen during the Civil War. At the end, the starving Royalist garrison was allowed to march out with full military honours. Victorian modifications included gun emplacements and a barracks, and the castle was also used for military purposes in both world wars.

South of the castle on the map lies the 'CG Station' or, more properly, the 'Maritime Rescue Co-ordination Centre Falmouth', whose area extends from the Cornwall/Devon border on the north coast to Dodman Point on the south, and out to 30°W, halfway across the Atlantic. The centre also acts as Britain's link with over 130 other nations in the international maritime rescue system.

Castle Drive continues high above the docks, which specialise in ship repair, and passes Falmouth Docks railway station, from where there are frequent services to Truro. Anchored in Carrick Roads you will sometimes see a large ocean-going tug, ready to dash to any ship in trouble, for a negotiable fee.

The path now follows Bar Road under the railway bridge, then Arwenack Street, Church Street and Market Street, to the Prince of Wales Pier and ferry to St Mawes. The new flagship building on the harbourside is the National Maritime Museum Cornwall **116**, with the national small boat collection. But there are also galleries showing Cornish maritime history and you can find out more about many of the topics touched on in this book. From the observation deck of the building's lighthouse-shaped tower you can look out over the harbour, and from the observation room at the bottom of the tower you can look out through the muddy waters of the harbour. Most of the building is made of concrete, but there is some granite, and Chinese, rather than Cornish, granite was chosen on the grounds of cost. Because of its strength and because it is possible to quarry large, flawless blocks, Cornish granite has played a disproportionate role not only in Cornwall's but in global maritime history. Lighthouses and harbours across the former British Empire, from Cork to Singapore, were made of Cornish granite (as were the docks of Buenos Aires and Copenhagen).

The final few hundred yards of this section of the South West Coast Path take you past many buildings whose stories not only encompass the short history of Falmouth but also resonate with many themes of the previous tens of miles. First is Arwenack, the former manor house of the Killigrew family who planned Falmouth, and across the road is the Killigrew Pyramid, built to beautify the harbour. Next is the Custom House **117** and the Pipe to burn contraband tobacco, then the parish church of King Charles the Martyr. A few yards on is Falmouth Arts Centre, the home of the Royal Cornwall Polytechnic Society, one of three historic bodies dating from the early 19th century. The other two are the Royal Institution of Cornwall (founded 1818), which runs the Royal Cornwall Museum in Truro, and the Royal Geological Society of Cornwall (founded 1814). Finally, squeezed up an alley opposite Marks and Spencer, is Bell's Court with two Elizabethan houses, one a working man's club, the other a shop but formerly housing the Cornwall Maritime Museum.

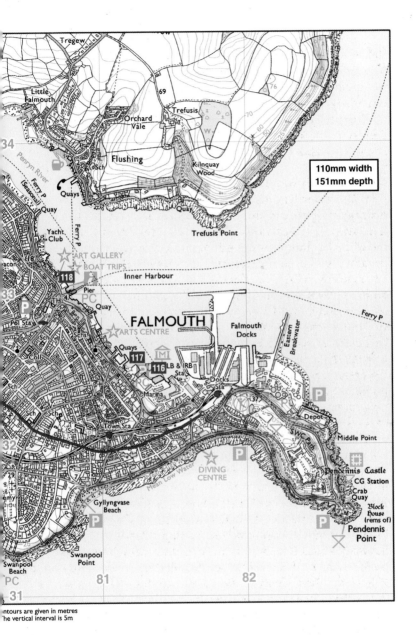

110mm width
151mm depth

Contours are given in metres
The vertical interval is 5m

From the Prince of Wales Pier on Albert Quay **118** the ferry leaves for St Mawes. Details of how to get there and then on to Place will be found on page 139. Now the Coast Path continues from Falmouth to Exmouth, as described in National Trail Guide no. 10.

Trinity House has provided a more reliable light at the Lizard than the Killigrews.

The Killigrews of Arwenack

The growth of Falmouth from two small fishing villages – Smithick and Pennycomequick – into a major port, eclipsing the far older ports of Penryn and Truro, was the work of the Killigrews, a family of whom it could well be said that they had their bread buttered on both sides. One of them spent time in the Fleet Prison, London, for piracy, and then later on became the first governor of Pendennis Castle. His son, also a temporary inhabitant of the Fleet, was Chairman of the Commission of Piracy in Cornwall and thus in charge of prose-cuting pirates. This proved fortunate for his wife, who led a gang to plunder a Spanish ship in the harbour and murder the crew; her accomplices were hanged. The grandson continued the entrepreneurial spirit by building the first Lizard light-house in 1619 as a money-making venture, but when he had trouble collecting the dues the light went out, much to the wreckers' benefit.

PART THREE

USEFUL
INFORMATION

Websites

The official website for the South West Coast Path National Trail is www.nationaltrail.co.uk/southwestcoastpath This is a comprehensive information source and incorporates the latest news about the path and links to travel and accommodation information.

Visit Cornwall's site, www.visitcornwall.com, has information about getting to Cornwall, accommodation and lots more.

Accessing the internet can be done from all Cornwall's public libraries, larger youth hostels and some tourist information centres. Internet cafes are rare, though Newquay has some.

Transport

Public transport in Cornwall is at its best in summer, but take care if you are told that there is a regular service: regular might mean once a week or term-time only. The main public transport information website for the SW, www.travelinesw.com , provides information about buses and trains (the information is also available by phone 0871 200 2233). Additionally, to help both visitors and residents alike, the Cornwall County Council Passenger Transport Unit (at County Hall, Truro, TR1 3AY. Tel: 01872 222000) publishes four excellent free Public Transport in Cornwall area guides. The guides for North, Mid and West Cornwall cover Padstow to Falmouth and you can order these by phone or email (ptu@cornwall.gov.uk), or collect from Tourist Information Centres and public libraries. The guides have details of all the air, bus and ferry services, with general information about trains, and are published in summer and winter editions each year. Operators can alter services with only six weeks' notice, and small supplements are published as necessary. Walkers may prefer to download the route map and relevant timetables from www.cornwallpublictransport.info

Two useful websites to find out options for travel within the UK are www.transportdirect.info and www.traveline.org.uk

Air

Newquay Airport has increasing links to the rest of the UK and beyond, and a bus link to Padstow and Newquay.

Rail

Frequent, regular and fast services connect Plymouth with the rest of Britain and Europe. Many of these services continue at a slower pace into Cornwall, at approximately hourly intervals, stopping at most of the stations on the main line, which ends at Penzance. Branch lines still connect Newquay, St Ives (change at St Erth or Penzance) and Falmouth (change at Truro) to the main line. Padstow is connected to the main line at Bodmin Parkway station by a bus. The major revisions of the railway timetable are made in May and December. or you can get information on www.nationalrail.co.uk from where you can also link to book tickets. There are three main ticket types: Advance, which must be bought in advance (up to 12 weeks ahead), with a seat reservation, and two which you can buy at any time: Off-Peak, where you travel off-peak, and Anytime where you travel any time. There are limited numbers of the cheap Advance tickets and they sell out fast. You can buy tickets on-line and collect them later from self-service ticket machine on many stations.

Buses

Long-distance coach services run by National Express connect Cornwall with the rest of Britain. National Express run direct services to Plymouth, London, Heathrow Airport, Bristol and the North. From Plymouth these National Express services link directly with various places on the Coast Path. The National Express enquiry line is 08717 818181, and the website is www.nationalexpress.co.uk Local services are provided by First Devon and Cornwall and several smaller operators. There are useful coastal links, mostly provided by Western Greyhound, which connect Padstow and Newquay, Newquay and St Ives, St Ives and St Just and Penzance. There are also services linking Penzance, Porthleven, the Lizard and Falmouth.

In remote areas you will see small signs with 'This way to the bus' fixed on existing signposts.

Ferries

Plymouth, on the coast path, is linked to Spain and France: you would then need to reach the Padstow – Falmouth section of the path by train, coach, bus or car.

Details of ferry services can be found on:
www.cornwallpublictransport.info
All ferries run only if the weather permits.

The Camel (Rock to Padstow)

This ferry runs every day in summer, but not on Sundays from the last Sunday in October to the first Sunday in April (unless Easter is early). The service is continuous, subject to demand, from 8.00 a.m. (from Padstow), with the last ferry from Rock leaving at 4.30 p.m. in the winter and at 7.30 p.m. in mid-summer, though 'the times of the last ferry are subject to variation with demand'; you may need to wave a green flag to summon the ferry. The ferry is operated by Padstow Harbour Commissioners, Harbour Office, Padstow, 01841 532239. You are strongly advised to contact the Harbour Office for up-to-date information, as the land route between Padstow and Rock is long and tortuous, and is ill-served by buses. A water taxi operates from Easter until the end of October, from 7 p.m. to midnight and then from 7.30 p.m. to midnight from mid July until the end of August. See www.rock-watertaxi.co.uk .

The Gannel

The far smaller Gannel Estuary is less of a problem with four bridges, three of which are tidal, and in summer one ferry service. The recommended crossing is over the tidal bridge straight across from Penpol Creek on the southern (Crantock) side. This is not usable for about half an hour (at neap tides) to 3 hours (at spring tides) either side of high water. The next tidal bridge upstream is near Trenance boating lake and is covered for about half an hour either side of high water but the path across the saltmarsh on the southern side may be flooded for longer. If you wish to cross the Gannel at high-water springs (morning and evening in Cornwall) you will need to use the Trevemper Bridge on the A3075. Finally, near the mouth of the Gannel there is a crossing point below the Fern Pit Café which is only available when the café is open, which is daily between 10 a.m. and 6 p.m. from Spring Bank Holiday to mid-September.

The ferry, tidal bridge and café are all owned and operated by the Northey family, Fern Pit, Riverside Crescent, Newquay, 01637 873181. On the Newquay side the crossing is linked to a private road by a private path through the café's garden and this path is only usable, in either direction, if the café is open. This ferry runs on demand but operations can be curtailed because of adverse sea and weather conditions.

The Helford

A ferry from Helford Point to Helford Passage runs between April 1 (or Good Friday if earlier) and October 31. The service runs daily on request from April 1 to October 31 from 9.30 to 5.30 and in July and August from 9.30am to 9.30 pm. Later or earlier can be arranged. The ferry is based at Helford Passage and can be contacted from Helford by swinging open the semi-circular blue board to show a yellow disc and the ferry will set off to pick you up. The service is run by Helford River Boats, 01326 250770, with a website www.helford-river-boats.co.uk The land route is well away from the side of the estuary, is around 14 miles (23 km) long and mostly on roads.

Carrick Roads (Falmouth to St Mawes)
There are ferries 364 days a year. The ferry runs from the Prince of Wales Pier off Albert Quay and times can be obtained from the operator, the St Mawes Ferry Company, 01872 861910 (office hours), or directly from the ferry (07855 438674) at other times, or from the website www.kingharryscornwall.co.uk

St Mawes to Place
The St Mawes Ferry Company also run to Place seven days a week from Good Friday to the end of October. Between November and April the options are to walk, to catch a bus and walk, or to take a taxi. The shortest route on foot, through St Just and Gerrans, is about 8 miles (13 km) long. Alternatively the harbourmaster or others in St Mawes will put you in touch with Truronian for details of the bus service between St Mawes and Portscatho.

Taxis
You can call the National Taxi Hotline free on 0800 654321 and you will be put in contact with the nearest taxi operator in the scheme. You can check the cost of your journey on the phone.

Accommodation

The major industry in Cornwall is tourism, so there is an abundance of places to stay: everything from expensive hotels with facilities you probably never dreamed you might need, to spare rooms in farmhouses and meals with the family in the kitchen; also self-catering holiday cottages, caravan parks, campsites and youth hostels. But out of season many of the places are shut and in a good season 'No Vacancies' signs are everywhere. It is also worth bearing in mind that it may be difficult to find accommodation for single nights at busy times. The route maps only show caravan and campsites with the relevant permission from the planning authority; complex planning rules allow other sites to be occupied for a maximum of 28 days per year. Summer visitors will find many of these sites, often with very basic facilities. Sites also set their own rules, which could, for example, mean the minimum stay is two nights, or only family groups are accepted.

The Tourist Information Centres can provide you with lists of places to stay, and for a small fee they will book accommodation at places on their registers. Registered places must meet certain standards, but many excellent B&Bs have not registered, so the fact that the Tourist Information Centre cannot book you a bed in, for example, Zennor does not mean either that there are no B&Bs in the area, or that they are not clean, warm and welcoming. If you are looking for accommodation it makes sense to purchase the annual guide, *The South West Coast Path*, published by the South West Coast Path Association. This lists places to stay, on or near the Coast Path, which welcome walkers. All entries have been recommended by walkers.

Tourist Information Centres on or near the section of Coast Path described in this book are listed below.

The Tourist Information Centre, The Red Brick Building, North Quay, Padstow PL28 8AF. Tel. 01841 533449.
Email: padstowtic@btconnect.com
Newquay's new Tourist Information Centre's location was not known in January 2009 but could be reached by email at contact@visitnewquay.org
The Tourist Information Centre, 5 Churchtown, St Agnes TR5 0QW. Tel. 01872 554150, Email: annetrevcott@aol.com
The Tourist Information Centre, The Guildhall, Street-an-Pol, St Ives TR26 2DS. Tel. 01736 796297.
Email: ivtic@penwith.gov.uk
The Tourist Information Centre, The Library, Market Street, St Just, Penzance TR19 7HX. Tel. 01736 788669.
Email: stjust.tic@btconnect.com
The Tourist Information Centre, Station Approach, Penzance TR18 2NF. Tel. 01736 362207. Email: pztic@penwith.gov.uk
The Tourist Information Centre, 11 Market Strand, Prince of Wales Pier, Falmouth TR11 3DF. Tel. 01326 312300.
Email: info@falmouthtic.co.uk

Both www.visitcornwall.com and www.visitsouthwest.co.uk will provide useful information about accommodation.

Other contacts

Camping and Caravanning Club, Greenfields House,
Westwood Way, Coventry, Warwickshire CV4 8JH.
Tel. 0845 130 7631. Site-list and map available to members.
Website: www.campingandcaravanningclub.co.uk

Caravan Club, East Grinstead House, East Grinstead, West
Sussex RH19 1UA. Tel. 01342 326944. Site-list and map
available to members. Website: www.caravanclub.co.uk

Ramblers' Association, 2nd Floor, Camelford House,
87–90 Albert Embankment, London SE1 7TW.
Tel. 020 7339 8500. Their website, www.ramblers.org.uk, has
a searchable accommodation finder available to the public.

South West Coast Path Association, Bowker House, Lee Mill
Bridge, Ivybridge, Devon PL21 9EF. Tel. 01752 896237. Annual
guide with many useful B&B addresses, available in
bookshops or free to members. Website: www.swcp.org.uk

YMCA, The Orchard, Alverton, Penzance, Cornwall TR18 4TE.
Tel. 01736 365016. This is the only residential YMCA centre
in the area.

Youth Hostels Association, Trevelyan House, Dimple Road,
Matlock DE4 3YH. Tel. 01629 592600. Annual handbook,
free to members. Groups might wish to rent a hostel when it
is normally closed out of the main season.
Website: www.yha.org.uk

Information about independent hostels can be found at
www.backpackers.co.uk

Baggage carrying and packaged walking holidays

Several firms operate guided and unguided walking holidays
along the Coast Path: there is a list of operators recommended by
South West Tourism on a link from the South West Coast Path
website, www.nationaltrail.co.uk/southwestcoastpath Some B&Bs
and hotels will deliver your luggage to your next overnight stop,
for a fee.

Other facilities

Refreshments

In summer you will find a great range of places to eat along or
near the coast. Out of season the choice is more restricted but
the growth of surfing has meant that many beachside places are
open through most of the year (the surf is better in winter).

Public conveniences

Many of the public conveniences shown on the maps are closed in winter, though when this is the case there is often a notice on the door showing the location of the nearest open one. But this information may be more useful for someone with a car.

Money

Withdrawing money in towns with banks should be no problem, but the number of banks is decreasing. Padstow, Newquay, St Ives, Penzance and Falmouth are the only towns where withdrawing money, from either a bank or an ATM (cash machine), should be no problem. ATMs are also being installed in shops and convenience stores but most of these make a charge for withdrawals, and in 2008 they worked for most, but not all, foreign banks. If your card has a Plus/Visa or Cirrus/Mastercard logo it should work in Link machines, the commonest ATMs in the UK: you can easily find their locations on the web at www.link.co.uk. Post offices have arrangements with several banks to facilitate withdrawals, but post offices are also decreasing in number. Many banks and post offices operate reduced hours out of season. Larger hotels, but not B&Bs, will usually take credit cards. Banks and larger post offices will change travellers' cheques. In emergency foreign visitors might wish to use the international MoneyGram transfer system available through larger post offices.

The advice has to be to ask your bank or building society, before you set out on the Coast Path, where you will be able to withdraw cash. Also to ask accommodation providers when you book how they wish to be paid.

Dogs

Many people take their dogs with them on the Coast Path. Responsible owners clean up dog mess no matter where they are, and put it in the bins provided. Owners are also required to keep their pets on leads in some places, and not let their animals disturb livestock, nesting birds or, indeed, other walkers. Farmers have the right to shoot any dogs disturbing livestock. Dogs are banned on many beaches in the season, but where the Coast Path crosses any such beach you have the right of direct passage with your dog, though of course it is advisable to put the animal on a short lead.

Books

Innumerable books and booklets have been published on Cornwall. Racks of booklets to tempt the tourist are in supermarkets, knick-knack shops, cafés, newsagents and bookshops, so there is no problem with getting information on everything from how to make clotted cream to smuggling. A series of reliable booklets on Cornwall's heritage (e.g. *Cornwall's Archaeological Heritage*) is published by Twelveheads Press, while more in-depth work is published by Cornish Hillside Press.

Ballantyne, R. M., *Deep Down* (1868, Diggory Press, 2005, 2006).

Bates, Robin and Scolding, Bill, *Beneath the Skin of The Lizard* (Cornwall County Council, 2000).

Bates, Robin and Scolding, Bill, *Wild Flowers of The Lizard* (Cornwall County Council, 2002).

Betjeman, J., *Betjeman's Cornwall* (Murray, 1984).

Bristow, Colin M., *Cornwall's Geology and Scenery* (Cornish Hillside, 1996, 2004).

Buckley, J. A., *The Cornish Mining Industry* (Tor Mark, 1992, 2002).

Brittain, Sarah, and Cook, Simon, *Behind the Canvas* (Truran, 2001).

Chapman, David, *Birds of Cornwall and the Isles of Scilly* (Alison Hodge, 2008).

Chapman, David, *Exploring the Cornish Coast* (Alison Hodge, 2008).

Chapman, David, *Wildflowers of Cornwall and the Isles of Scilly* (Alison Hodge, 2008).

Cornwall Archaeological Unit, *Cornwall's Archaeological Heritage* (Twelveheads Press, 1990, 2003).

Cross, Tom, *Painting the Warmth of the Sun – St Ives Artists 1939–1975* (Alison Hodge and Lutterworth Press, 1984).

Cross, Tom, *The Shining Sands – Artists in Newlyn and St Ives 1880–1930* (Lutterworth, 1994).

Cross, Tom, *Catching the Wave – Artists in Newlyn and St Ives 1975–The Present* (Halsgrove, 2002).

Davidson, Alan, *North Atlantic Seafood* (Macmillan, 1979; Penguin, 1980).

Dines, H. G., *The Metalliferous Mining Region of South-West England* (HMSO, 1956 and 1988).

Embrey, P. G. and Symes, R. F., *Minerals of Cornwall and Devon* (British Museum Natural History and Mineralogical Record Inc., 1987).

Goode, Tony, Holder, Martin and Leveridge, Brian, *West Cornwall – A Landscape for Leisure* (British Geological Survey, 1996).

Harris, K., *Hevva! Cornish Fishing in the Days of Sail* (Truran, 1983).

Holmes, J., *1000 Cornish Place Names Explained* (Truran, 2000).

Kent, Alan M. (transl.), *The Ordinalia* (Francis Boutle, 2005).

Kittridge, Alan, *Cornwall's Maritime Heritage* (Twelveheads Press, 1989, 2003).

Lawman, Jean, *A Natural History of the Lizard Peninsula* (Truran and the Institute of Cornish Studies, 1994).

Lawman, Jean, *A Natural History of Land's End* (Tabb House, Padstow, 2002).

Mabey, Richard, *Food for Free* (Collins, 1972 and 1989).

National Trust *Coast of Cornwall* Series (10 leaflets cover the area between Padstow and Falmouth).

Padel, O. J., A *Popular Dictionary of Cornish Place-Names* (Alison Hodge, 1988).

Pevsner, N., and revised by same and Enid Radcliffe, *Cornwall – The Buildings of England* (Penguin, 1951 and 1970).

Rowse, A. L., *A Cornish Anthology* (Macmillan, 1968; Alison Hodge, 1982 and 1990).

Stanier, Peter H., *Cornwall's Literary Heritage* (Twelveheads Press, 1992).

Stanier, Peter H., *Cornwall's Mining Heritage* (Twelveheads Press, 1988, 2002).

Tangye, Michael, *Tehidy and the Bassets* (Truran, 1984, 2002).

Tarrant, Michael, *Cornwall's Lighthouse Heritage* (Twelveheads Press, 1990, 2007).

Thomas, D. M. (ed.), *The Granite Kingdom: Poems of Cornwall* (D. Bradford Barton, 1970).

Waugh, Mary, *Smuggling in Devon & Cornwall* (Countryside, 1991).

Woolf, Virginia, *To the Lighthouse* (Hogarth Press, 1927).

Ordnance Survey Maps covering the South West Coast Path (Padstow to Falmouth)

Landranger Maps (1:50000): 200, 203, 204

Explorer Maps (1:25000):

    102 (Land's End, Penzance & St Ives)

    103 (The Lizard, Falmouth & Helston)

    104 (Redruth & St Agnes)

    106 (Newquay & Padstow)